For NORB —

loved those HOT

Hillary xxxx nights...

Xxe Twins

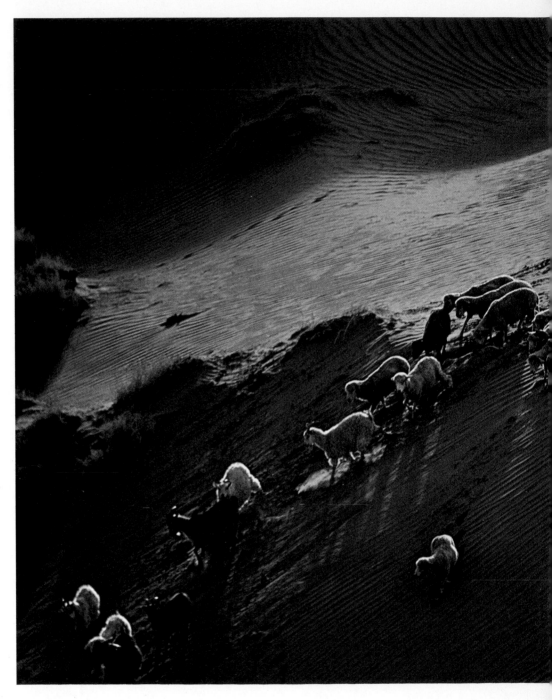

By Rowe Findley
Photographed by Walter Meayers Edwards
Foreword by Edmund C. Jaeger

Prepared by the Special Publications Division,
National Geographic Society,
Washington, D. C.

Great American Deserts

GREAT AMERICAN DESERTS
By ROWE FINDLEY
National Geographic Senior Editorial Staff
Photographed by WALTER MEAYERS EDWARDS
National Geographic Staff

Published by
THE NATIONAL GEOGRAPHIC SOCIETY
MELVIN M. PAYNE, *President*
MELVILLE BELL GROSVENOR, *Editor-in-Chief*
GILBERT M. GROSVENOR, *Editor*
ROBERT PAUL JORDAN, *Consulting Editor*

Prepared by
THE SPECIAL PUBLICATIONS DIVISION
ROBERT L. BREEDEN, *Editor*
DONALD J. CRUMP, *Associate Editor*
PHILIP B. SILCOTT, *Senior Assistant Editor*
RONALD M. FISHER, WILLIAM R. GRAY, H. ROBERT
    MORRISON, CYNTHIA RUSS RAMSAY, *Assistants to
    the Editor*
CYNTHIA RUSS RAMSAY, ANN C. RESH, MARGARET L.
    DUGDALE, MARGERY G. DUNN, JOHANNA G. FARREN,
    TEE LOFTIN SNELL, PATRICIA G. TOWLE, *Research*
Illustrations
WILLIAM L. ALLEN, *Picture Editor*
ROBERT COCHRAN, MARGERY G. DUNN, WILLIAM
    R. GRAY, ROY HOOPES, STRATFORD C. JONES,
    H. ROBERT MORRISON, *Picture Legends*

Layout and Design
JOSEPH A. TANEY, *Staff Art Director*
JOSEPHINE B. BOLT, *Art Director*
URSULA PERRIN, *Design Assistant*
JOHN D. GARST, JR., VIRGINIA L. BAZA,
    Map Research and Production

Production and Printing
ROBERT W. MESSER, *Production Manager*
MARGARET MURIN SKEKEL, RAJA D. MURSHED,
    Production Assistants
JAMES R. WHITNEY, JOHN R. METCALFE, *Engraving
    and Printing*
MARTA I. BERNAL, TONI EUGENE, SUZANNE J.
    JACOBSON, ELIZABETH VAN BEUREN JOY,
    JOAN PERRY, *Staff Assistants*
ANNE MCCAIN, TONI WARNER, *Index*

Standard Book Number 87044-107-8
Library of Congress Catalog Card Number 72-75382

Overleaf: *Heading for sparse pasture, Navajo women and children
herd sheep and goats across wind-rippled dunes in Monument Valley,
a broad, sloping land on the Arizona-Utah line. Much tribal income
depends on the sale of meat and wool. Page 1: A desert blossom spreads
delicate petals among the spiny armaments of a cactus plant. Bookbinding: Fleet of foot, a roadrunner sprints across the desert floor.*
OVERLEAF: NATIONAL GEOGRAPHIC PHOTOGRAPHER BRUCE DALE;
PAGE 1: BILL RATCLIFFE; BOOKBINDING: DRAWING BY CHARLES MURPHY

WILLIS PETERSON

Shaded *by a prickly pear, a black-tailed jackrabbit waits out the
heat. Interlaced with blood vessels, the large thin ears serve a
double purpose: They help the hare dissipate body heat and help
provide it with acutely sensitive hearing to warn of danger.*

FOR 65 YEARS now I have loved the desert. I first saw it from the windows of a train, traveling from Nebraska to California with my parents. My father needed a change of climate for his health. It was 1906, the year of the San Francisco earthquake, and the ground was still trembling there when we reached California. Of the desert we crossed I remember wide expanses of creosote bush, great sandy washes, and Indians standing on the platform at Yuma.

A few years later, when I was still a young man, I climbed more than 10,000 feet to the peak of Mount San Jacinto and saw the desert spread below me. I felt its vastness and solitude—and beauty—tugging at me, and I vowed then and there that one day I would know it. For 30 years I was a Professor of Zoology at City College in Riverside, California, and I spent nearly every weekend and holiday camping in the desert with my students.

I remember campsites rimmed with beds of sand verbenas and evening primroses, smoke tree washes and sagebrush valleys. I remember riding a burro into Palm Springs, at the edge of the desert, where I began teaching. There were 40 registered voters there, mostly Indians. Now, of course, it's a plush resort. And I remember waking at dawn and seeing a coyote playing with a piece of canvas from our camping equipment, tossing it and tugging it, frolicking like a puppy. He ran right across the chest of my sleeping companion and began cavorting with some crumpled wastepaper we were saving for our morning fire. He was not in the least bothered by our presence. I have great admiration for the coyote, for in spite of all the persecutions of man, and all the hardships he must endure, still he thrives.

Water is the life of the desert. There are desert animals that never need a drink of water. There are desert seeds that can wait 15 to 20 years for rainfall. That to me is one of the wonders of life. A seed no larger than a period on this page can hold all of a plant's possibilities, waiting. No thinking man can fail to be awed by the mystery of it.

There is only one way really to see the desert, and that is on foot, away from the highways. The desert of people is not my desert. I want open space. I want to see the animals and flowers of the desert, to hear the sounds of the dry, whistling winds, and the insects and the birds. The desert is largely a land of silence, but if you listen you can hear it.

I'm glad that I've lived during the period that I have, for I saw California when it was young, and I saw the deserts in their pristine state. All my life I have enjoyed the boundless solitude and space. In just the past 30 years, huge areas of desert lands, watered by man-made reservoirs and opened by roads, have become home to millions. Many have exploited the deserts as a source of quick riches from minerals, land speculation, overbuilding, careless recreation. While it seems inevitable that desert areas will be put to man's physical use more and more in the next decades, I hope some significant portion will be preserved in its natural state for the soul of man. This intelligent and perceptive book should help inspire us toward that goal. Just as deserts have long been a source of great joy to me, I know they can be for thousands of others. We need only approach them on their own terms—and with great reverence.

EDMUND C. JAEGER, Sc.D., LL.D.
Professor Emeritus
Riverside City College, California

Moments *before sunset, a dust cloud settles slowly around tall saguaros after a violent windstorm in Sonora, Mexico. This land, often barren in appearance, "requires time to be comprehended," says geographer Stephen C. Jett. "For someone*

Contents

*who is unused to the scale of the south-
western landscape, comprehension requires waiting, wandering, wondering;
for such landscapes are at first hardly
believable, impossible to absorb at a
single sitting...."*

Land of Big Skies And Big Horizons

THE MOVING LIGHT OF DAWN finds the desert a piece at a time, first touching the highest peaks with orange while the rest of the world waits beneath a sea of blue half-light. I remember especially an April morning when my wife Virginia and I walked into the deepening indigo of an Arizona canyon just as the first early-bird songs were being ventured. Moments later, the sun discovered the skymost crags above us, sending a mellow glow among the canyon's spiny cactus forest of organ pipes, saguaros, and chollas. Dipping down the chasm's rocky sides, the sun at last sought out a cluster of paloverde trees in fullest bloom, golden fleece against a purple-shadowed stone backdrop. "Could anything be more beautiful?" Virginia asked. I thought not.

We would know so many moments of stunning lights and haunting panoramas in our desert travels, however, that comparisons would drown in richness. Yet the excitement and beauty of desert lands go far beyond the mere experience to a sense of their vital place in the scheme of our world. Vaulting stone arches, striped buttes, huge mesas, and fragile spires bear vivid witness to the power of erosion that wears our continents down. Cinder-heaped volcano fields and great fault-lifted mountains testify to the dynamic forces that are building the continents up again. The resourceful kangaroo rat and hardy creosote bush tell of life's ability to endure and thrive in a harsh realm. The ranchers and prospectors and boomers and dreamers bear witness to the self-reliance born of necessity, of cheer tinged sometimes with desperation, of schemes as wild as the land itself.

Some of my friends think my love of such country is a bit wild too. Here's the picture that often comes to their minds at mention of the word "desert":

Glaring sun . . . seas of dunes shimmering in heat waves toward distant salt flats . . . the wind erasing a zigzag of footprints . . . another victim swallowed up.

Some of my desert friends tend to be too enthusiastic in the other direction. They talk in terms of Shangri-Las where health is automatically assured.

Obviously, desert means different things to different people, and the truth lies somewhere between opinion's extremes. I confess my own surprise when, many years ago, military service brought me to southern New Mexico, where I first fell under the desert spell. There I found that the Sahara image of endless dunes applied to but a tiny fraction of the terrain. It's also true that winds blow awesomely, but I remember great chains of calm, mild days. *(Continued on page 16)*

Darkness settles about campers at Cabo San Lucas on the southern tip of Baja California. Desert fringes the mountainous spine of the peninsula, once isolated by poor roads. Now increasing miles of paved highway bring an end to the region's seclusion and hasten development.
BEE PLANT (CLEOME SERRULATA), BILL RATCLIFFE (UPPER); WILLIAM BELKNAP, JR.

"Sky City" of Acoma, one of the oldest continuously occupied villages in the U.S., huddles atop its butte more than 350 feet above the plain west of Albuquerque, New Mexico. Since the early 13th century, Pueblo Indians have lived

ADAM WOOLFITT

here, descending to work their fields —
and they still graze livestock introduced
by the Spanish.

Flat face *of Nevada's Reese River Valley sprouts a stubble of shadscale—a low shrub common on alkaline plains and dry mesas from Oregon to Mexico. Autumn snow clouds roll toward the desert over the Toiyabe Range.*

Shimmering lake—*a tantalizing mirage—reflects trees growing near Baker, California. The optical illusion results from light bending as it passes from one layer of air to another of different density. Although associated with hot, dry regions, mirages have occurred at sea, and during cool weather. "This one really surprised me," recalled National Geographic's photographer Walter Meayers Edwards. "The temperature that day was only about 50 degrees."*

Headlights on *and windows shut, a school bus heads through a sandstorm near Desert Center, California. More frequent in spring, such storms can reduce visibility to zero, etch windshields to frosted glass, and sandblast paint from car bodies. In periods of severe wind, drifting keeps road graders busy and may even block highways, sometimes for days.*

SAM ABELL (ABOVE)

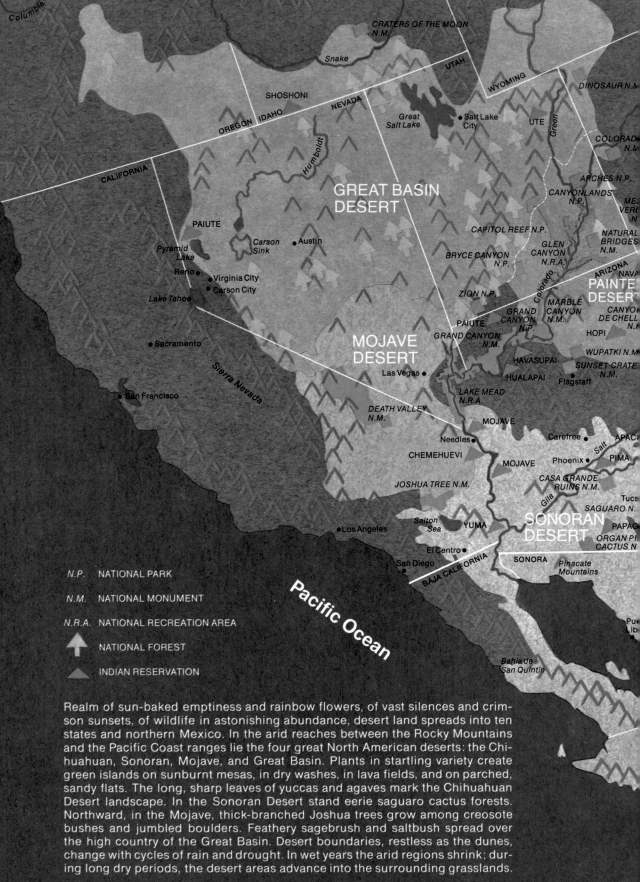

Realm of sun-baked emptiness and rainbow flowers, of vast silences and crimson sunsets, of wildlife in astonishing abundance, desert land spreads into ten states and northern Mexico. In the arid reaches between the Rocky Mountains and the Pacific Coast ranges lie the four great North American deserts: the Chihuahuan, Sonoran, Mojave, and Great Basin. Plants in startling variety create green islands on sunburnt mesas, in dry washes, in lava fields, and on parched, sandy flats. The long, sharp leaves of yuccas and agaves mark the Chihuahuan Desert landscape. In the Sonoran Desert stand eerie saguaro cactus forests. Northward, in the Mojave, thick-branched Joshua trees grow among creosote bushes and jumbled boulders. Feathery sagebrush and saltbush spread over the high country of the Great Basin. Desert boundaries, restless as the dunes, change with cycles of rain and drought. In wet years the arid regions shrink; during long dry periods, the desert areas advance into the surrounding grasslands.

Great American Deserts

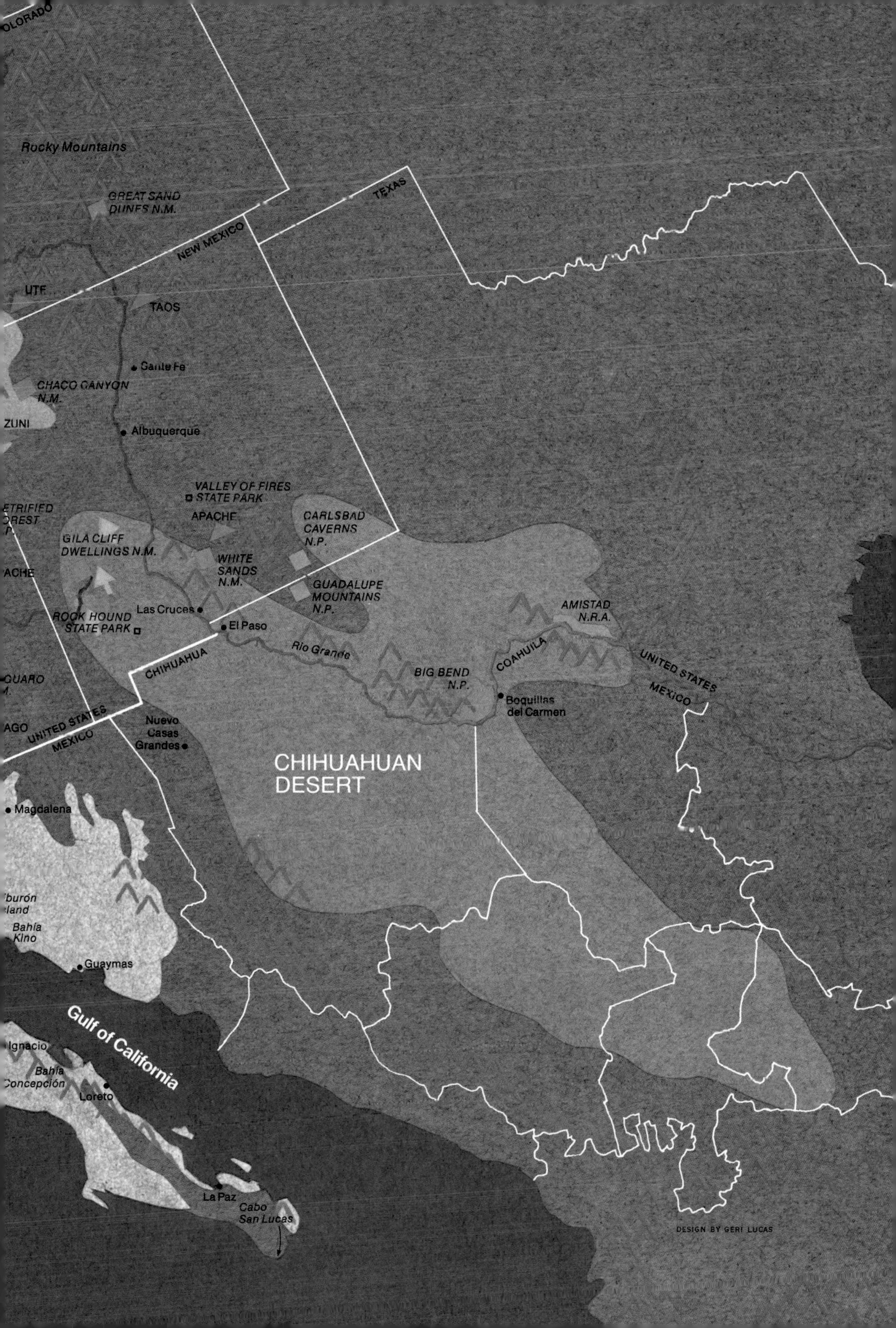

Rocky Mountains

GREAT SAND
DUNES N.M.

COLORADO

TEXAS

NEW MEXICO

UTE

TAOS

• Santa Fe

CHACO CANYON
N.M.

ZUNI

• Albuquerque

VALLEY OF FIRES
STATE PARK

ETRIFIED
OREST
P.

APACHE

CARLSBAD
CAVERNS
N.P.

GILA CLIFF
DWELLINGS N.M.

WHITE
SANDS
N.M.

ACHE

GUADALUPE
MOUNTAINS
N.P.

AMISTAD
N.R.A.

ROCK HOUND
STATE PARK

Las Cruces •

• El Paso

Rio Grande

COAHUILA

UNITED STATES

CUARO
M.

CHIHUAHUA

BIG BEND
N.P.

MEXICO

AGO

UNITED STATES

MEXICO

Nuevo
Casas
Grandes •

• Boquillas
del Carmen

CHIHUAHUAN
DESERT

• Magdalena

burón
land

Bahía
Kino

• Guaymas

Gulf of California

Ignacio

Bahía
Concepción

• Loreto

La Paz •

Cabo
San Lucas

DESIGN BY GERI LUCAS

People fear desert heat, and rightly so, but we found cold to be more of a problem. I've awakened in late April in southern Utah to find my sleeping bag under an icy mantle of snow, and Virginia and I were glad we had roaring campfires and snug down-filled sleeping bags for February nights on the quarter-mile-high desert of central Baja California.

Though many people have met tragic death in the desert, many more have come to the arid land and regained health. And just as there is something in the clear dry air that may restore the body, there is something in its ever-changing lights, stubborn life, and distant skylines that exhilarates the spirit. "It's a country where you can see clear into forever," said El Paso artist Russell R. Waterhouse, whose perceptive brush captures the land's big sky.

There was a time not so long ago when Virginia had her doubts about deserts. "I'm a mountain person," she said, and by that she meant green mountains—like the Great Smokies or the forested slopes of the Rockies.

The fact that mountain ranges generously corrugate North American deserts, with many rooftop forests of pine and aspen and fir, did much to help me change Virginia's tolerance for arid country to a growing affection. Then California's Death Valley, of all places, completed the conversion.

You see, Death Valley is really a very lively place. There's a date-palm-shaded oasis called Furnace Creek, with store, cabins, swimming pools, stables, and a clientele of desert-loving folk. Stretching upward from the lowest point in the Americas, 282 feet below sea level, surrounding mountains rise abruptly, one to 11,049 feet, wearing bristlecone pines and covered with snow much of the year. Death Valley made Virginia a mountain-*and-desert* person, as it did our sons David, 17, Steve, 14, and John, 7, who accompanied us during part of our travels.

In 25,000 miles of travel we visited North America's four major arid regions, the Sonoran, Mojave, Great Basin, and Chihuahuan Deserts, along with many of their extensions and subdivisions. We poked into ghost towns, found old-timers in reminiscent moods, learned much from botanists and zoologists, questioned geologists about the distinctive look of the land, chased mirages, slid down dunes, and rode desert-river rapids. We'd like to start tomorrow and do it all over again.

For pioneers moving west, the first problem the deserts presented was simply their location. Lt. Zebulon Pike in 1806 and Maj. Stephen Long 15 years later explored the Great Plains and agreed independently that the area was a vast desolation. Major Long called it "uninhabitable." Mapmakers labeled the region "Great American Desert," a name that stuck for half a century, discouraging settlement on soil that would become a granary for the Nation.

Still, that granary has had its problems, because it lies in a drought-ridden transition zone separating the well-watered Midwest from the desert Southwest.

More or less perpetual drought marks the true desert. I remember the shock I felt upon learning that in all the 770-mile length of Baja California, not one year-round stream really worthy of the name river flows into the sea.

Most of that peninsula lies in the low, stony Sonoran Desert, which also takes in the Mexican state of Sonora and spreads northward into southern California and Arizona. Despite its harshness, plants abound, especially where the land rises to one or two or three thousand feet, as it does along the central spine of Baja California and around Tucson. Cactus trees—saguaros in Arizona and cardons farther south—rule over great spreads of vegetation: paloverdes, mesquites, agaves, lesser cactus species, ocotillos, and occasional gray-green wispy smoke trees. "I tell my friends around Tucson that they live in a jungle," joked Mrs. Karen Fowler, director of the new Living Desert Reserve, near Palm Desert, California.

Not far north of her home begins the Mojave Desert, which lies between the Sonoran to its south and east and the lofty Great Basin Desert to its northeast. Joshua trees dominate its sparser plant life. At its eastern edge lies Death Valley.

Though the Great Basin Desert has rivers, few of them escape to the sea. Most are doomed to waste away into desert flats, unless some farmer's thirsty irrigated fields blot them up first. I've followed more than one brash brook tumbling out of a canyon, only to see it quickly shrink to a mere dark stain on the sands. Nevada lies almost wholly within this desert and, except where the Colorado River's Lake Mead washes its foot and where the tributaries of the Snake River flow northward into Idaho, the state swallows all its own rivers into sinks or saline lakes. Sagebrush and shrubs cover its valleys, and many of its mountains rise high enough to support coniferous forest.

The desert I came to know first was the Chihuahuan. That's the one that covers a large triangular plateau in northern Mexico and reaches across west Texas into the river valleys of southern New Mexico. "It's the continent's most isolated desert," chief naturalist Ro Wauer of Big Bend National Park told us. "It has more endemic varieties of plants and animals than others—the Sierra del Carmen deer, for example, in the mountain range just east of the park. There are at least 60 cactus varieties, including three that we're still trying to classify."

Though our desert loyalties began with the land itself, they now spring just as strongly from the special people we met there.

We met Marta Becket, who performs ballet-pantomime in her own theater in the town of Death Valley Junction, and her husband Tom Williams, who supports her solo performances by serving as master of ceremonies, lighting director, stagehand, and—on more than one night during their early days in the unusual venture—the only pair of hands to applaud her. "At first the desert was just a place to try our dream," Marta told us, "but now we've come to love it."

And how did New York-born Marta and Madison-Avenue-fugitive Tom come to Death Valley Junction? A concert tour brought them there in 1967, and a flat tire stopped them there. While Tom saw to repairs, Marta looked around the dusty plaza and found an abandoned community hall and movie house.

"To me it was an opera house where I could create and perform the kind of dances that expressed what I felt," she said. So Tom and Marta leased the building and named it the Amargosa Opera House. Now Marta's talents win increasing acclaim from appreciative audiences.

We met people like Bill Belknap of Boulder City, Nevada, outdoorsman, photographer, and writer, who loves the desert's freedom and dislikes restrictions imposed in the name of caution. "A man should be free to climb a mountain and maybe get himself killed without having to apply for a permit," Bill says.

We met Merle and Margaret Stockman of Oregon and Death Valley, who will drive a hundred miles to enjoy a field of desert flowers or seek a glimpse of a bighorn sheep. Merle provides me with little-suspected facts, like the news in a recent letter that it had taken Death Valley 60 years to get 100 inches of rain.

Because distances are wide and people seldom get together in big numbers, exuberance sometimes takes over when they do congregate. I'm thinking of two wild events in particular—Death Valley's Burro Flapjack Sweepstakes, part of the modern forty-niners' annual reunion, and Terlingua's chili cook-off, billed as the

Overleaf: Mountain lion faces 35 pounds of trouble—a snarling badger. When a handler freed the captive animals for a time in the Mojave Desert, they reacted instinctively. Surprised while digging by a Joshua tree, the badger crouched to attack; the 90-pound cat turned and ran.

world series of chili concoction. In both instances, thousands come to cheer events that make no sense except as extravagant nonsense. No prospector of old ever persuaded his "desert canary" to race with full pack around a pylon, then rammed a half-cooked pancake down that self-willed creature's gullet, yet that is the essence of the flapjack event. No west Texas quicksilver miner ever challenged the world to a chili-making competition, yet that is what happens in the little mercury ghost town today, while bands play and starlets pose for photographers.

We got to the Terlingua affair too late to sample any of the chili, so we went on down the road a few miles to visit old-timer Carl Thain. Like many others we met, Carl used hearty humor and brusque words to mask a tenderness for the desert country. "You've got to have water to do anything with this land," he told us. "Without water, you couldn't take two desert rats and a quart of whiskey and raise hell on it." He was proud of a well that had given him sweet water at about 830 feet, even though it had cost him in the neighborhood of $5,000.

In Riverside, California, I talked with Dr. Edmund Jaeger, at 85 the author of several books on North American deserts and the dean of this country's desert naturalists. He is concerned about the increasing pressures that rising populations have put on deserts in his lifetime. "When I first rode a burro to Palm Springs in 1915—to teach five children in a one-room school—there was only one house on the road to Indio," he said. "Today about 100,000 people live along that road, and when you drive it, it's hard to see open country on either side."

The mixed blessings of air conditioning and four-wheel drive worry Dr. Jaeger, because they allow people to penetrate once-inhospitable areas in comfort. "We mustn't use up all our open space," he said. "If we spoil our desert in pursuit of recreation, then there will be true recreation in the desert for no one."

The message is getting through to increasing numbers, partly because of such institutions as the Arizona-Sonora Desert Museum near Tucson. More than 300,000 people a year see its cactus garden, vampire bats, underwater views into the worlds of the otter and beaver, and its unusual tunnel where visitors can peer into the burrows of kit foxes and prairie dogs and ring-tailed cats.

The best way to appreciate the land is to get out into it, of course, and that's what we did—afoot and by mule, by boat and plane. We even desert-tested a modern covered wagon, a 27-foot Holiday Rambler travel trailer, but mostly we relied on our four-wheel-drive Travelall—and we always packed plenty of supplies.

The desert world is an intoxicating one of silence and solitude that treats you to midday dust devils dancing through mirages, sunset peaks touched with alpenglow, and midnights when the stars seem to touch the canyon rims. I remember one night when clouds suddenly blotted out the moon, and a few growling gusts of wind carried the smell of rain that never reached the ground. Then, as the squall retreated, I saw a moonbow form and float like a spectral bridge in the sky.

Next morning the memory of it was like the mirages we could never overtake, or the breeze-borne hints of fragrance from flowers never found.

Yet floods of other moments come back as real as the bacon and biscuits we breakfasted on that sun-bright Utah morning—the stinging needles of sand on the move in the wind, a Nevada mountain camp's heady mix of juniper smoke and boiling coffee at dawn, the rasping rollicking joy of an old fiddler's hoedown in the velvet evening of Death Valley. In memory, I am enchanted with deserts.

Performing a ballet-pantomime, Marta Becket dances in the Amargosa Opera House, Death Valley Junction, California. In 1967 she discovered an old movie house there and determined to live in the desert. On the walls she painted an audience of 16th-century Spaniards.

Rafting down the Green River in Canyonlands National Park, Utah, vacationists towing small fiberglass Sportyaks keep close to water—one of the desert's scarcest resources. Later, they may launch their bathtub fleet for bucking rides through canyon rapids. Above the river, on progressively drier terraces and canyon slopes, the fringe of willows and poplars soon gives way to sparse shrubs.

Swimmers splash in the Great Salt Lake near Magna, Utah, at Silver Sands Beach. Beyond rise smokestacks of a Kennecott Copper Corporation smelting plant. The company removes sulphur gases from the stack emissions, converts them into sulphuric acid, and markets the reclaimed product.

Fresh breeze speeds land sailors around a marker on a race course at El Mirage Dry Lake, California. The lightweight craft, made of hollow steel tubing with dacron sails, can tack like sailboats and travel at more than twice the speed of the wind. Experienced sailors reach 60 miles an hour or more.

Alert roadrunner, *fastest American bird afoot, stands still for a moment beside a beavertail cactus. Able to sprint at least 15 miles an hour, it easily outraces its prey: lizards, young rattlesnakes, insects, and spiders.*

Wings spread *forward, an osprey brakes to a landing on its nest near Puerto Libertad, Sonora, Mexico. Here the Gulf of California laps at the edge of the desert, providing a fishing ground for the high-diving osprey. Its nest, a platform of sticks, rests high in a cardon cactus. One of the largest cactus species in North America, the cardon sometimes grows 60 feet tall.*

Well adapted *to a harsh environment, desert plants exhibit astonishing variety. The leafy ocotillo, dagger-sharp lechuguilla, and prickly pear cactus (left) grow within inches of each other in the Chihuahuan Desert region of southwest Texas. They sprout from a sloping area covered with a mosaic of stones that form desert pavement. The crust forms as wind or rain removes soil from around and beneath stones, and they gradually settle and become wedged firmly together.*

Touching Hands With History

AT TAOS PUEBLO in New Mexico it was a big oval loaf of crusty bread still warm from a beehive oven that gave us the flavor of history; at San Ignacio in Baja California it was a glass of deep-red grape wine, from vines first planted by rugged Jesuit padres.

Indian bread, Spanish wine . . . Indian and Spaniard . . . two diverse peoples who met and fought and finally blended into a colorful desert lands civilization that prizes rain dances and bullfights, tom-toms and guitars. To find out more about some of today's desert people, and through their lives catch glimpses into the past, my wife Virginia and I set out to meet as many of them as we could.

For a starting place we went to a beach-scalloped sweep of Sonoran seacoast where some 370 Seri Indians still live in small, semi-nomadic groups. There we met Chico Romero, who claimed to have seen 107 summers, oldest man in the tribe.

"My hide is tough—like the coyote's," the ancient Indian told us. There was pride in his low voice, and the hint of a chuckle. Like the coyote, he'd lived much of his life under the sky, exposed to the elements. To get the next meal, he'd often had to scramble and use his wits, again like the coyote, who stars in dry-country mythology as a wily clown, a conniver for the easy life.

From Bahía Kino north, a 90-mile stretch of mountainous shore is home to the Seris, a people with one foot on the desert and one in the sea. They have no ancestral memory of any other home, and once they roved more of the mainland and offshore Tiburón Island as well. From the sea they harvest sharks and turtles. From the land they gather cactus fruit, bean-laden honey mesquite pods, and hearts of agaves. In either element they know the peril that even one mischance can bring.

Chico recalls when the agave saved the lives of a small party marooned on waterless San Esteban Island. The Indians, four or five adults and a boy, had beached their boat to hunt an agave that grows only there and on one other island. "Their boat was set adrift by unfriendly fishermen," Chico said. "They cooked and pounded the agave leaves and got juice to drink. They made a balsa [boat] out of the stalks, and one man and the boy went for help. Rescuers came in time to save them all. This happened when I was a boy."

To hear more about the Seris, we followed a two-track sand and gravel road that wound over mountain shoulders studded with giant cardon cactus and along sloping seaside plains abloom with crimson ocotillo. *(Continued on page 32)*

Seri Indian *Ignacio Molino, one of a tribe of fewer than 400, sits in a makeshift tent where he sells ironwood carvings to tourists. The Seris, who formerly subsisted mainly by fishing, live along the Gulf of California in Sonora, Mexico—the tribal homeland for two millenniums.*
CARDON CACTUS (PACHYCEREUS PRINGLEI), WILLIAM BELKNAP, JR. (UPPER); VIRGINIA FINDLEY

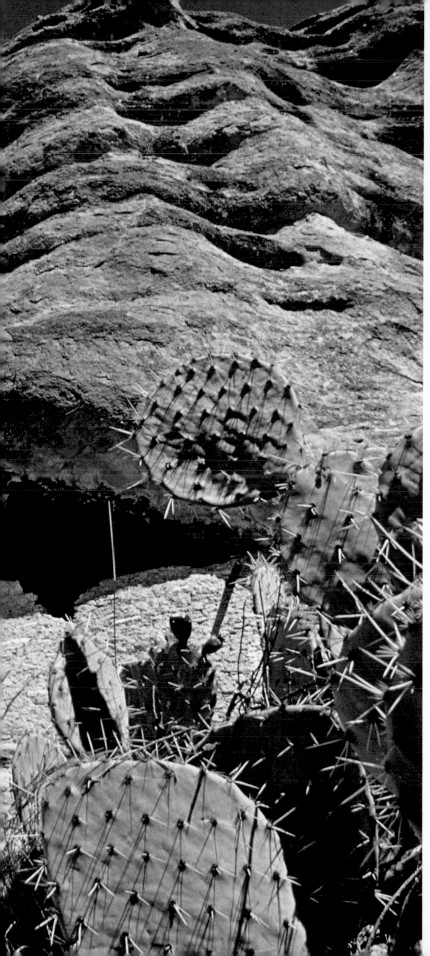

Chiseled *a thousand years ago by an Indian artist, a petroglyph near the Colorado River in Utah depicts a 4½-inch-high figure with out-size hands. Lake Powell—a snaking, 186-mile-long waterway impounded by Glen Canyon Dam for power, flood control, and recreation—has drowned this and hundreds of other figures and designs.*

Natural cave *in a sandstone canyon shelters a 13th-century ruin in New Mexico's Gila Cliff Dwellings National Monument. Built of adobe, mud, and stone, it housed Indian farmers who raised squash, beans, and corn on mesa tops and stream bottomlands; they supplemented this diet with game and wild nuts and fruit such as that from the prickly pear. By 1400 they had abandoned their fields and dwellings and mysteriously disappeared.*

29

Adobe labyrinth of Casas Grandes — Spanish for "big houses" — sprawls on a sun-washed plain in Chihuahua. Metropolis of an Indian civilization that existed between 1050 and 1340, the city covered about 90 acres and housed perhaps 5,000 people. Highly urbanized, the Casas Grandians constructed large temples, wide plazas, and multistory apartments. A network of dams and ditches controlled the meager water supply, channeling some to the city and diverting the rest to irrigate thousands of square miles of arid land. Casas Grandians also crafted highly detailed pottery; archeologist Charles C. Di Peso (lower left), head of excavations at the city, examines pots with human and animal designs. Despite its advanced culture, the city collapsed into ruin, possibly from invasion or revolt.

Kivas — underground ceremonial chambers — pock the floor of Pueblo Bonito in New Mexico's Chaco Canyon National Monument. A structure of 650 rooms tiered in places to four levels, the city that the Spanish named "beautiful village" provided housing for 1,000 people at its zenith more than 900 years ago. Between the 10th and 14th centuries, thousands of Indian communities — from cities like Casas Grandes and Pueblo Bonito to small settlements of three or four families — dotted the sere lands of the southwest.

Our goal was Desemboque, the remote home of an unusual American couple.

For 20 years Edward and Mary B. (Becky) Moser have dwelt with the Seris, studying their language and learning how they live. The Mosers are members of the Summer Institute of Linguistics, and their primary task is to translate parts of the Bible into Seri. But they're also observing and recording the Seri way of life.

"The Seris have songs about the desert heat," Becky told us. "One says that the heat is so intense that it has sound. The sound has spirit power. A woman fears the heat and won't go out in it to gather the cactus fruit. Her basket chides her, declaring that it is eager to get out into the heat."

To translate the Bible, the Mosers first had to devise a written language for the Seris. They did it with a Roman alphabet, using 19 consonant sounds and 4 vowels. "We can teach a Seri to read in only a few days," Ed told us.

As we left the Mosers, they gave Virginia a necklace of dried desert flowers. "If you put them in water they will open up again," Becky said. Someday, when Seri country seems too far away, I'll ask Virginia to moisten the tiny petals so that we can have a desert bouquet.

Returning along the coast, we bargained with long-haired, long-skirted Seri women at a beachside camp for ironwood carvings of birds, turtles, fish, and I bought a shark. Near a fisherman's hut, three real sharks, just caught, lay belly-up on the sand. An oniony turtle stew bubbled on the fire.

Hunting bigger game than fish or jackrabbits posed a challenge for desert Indians when they had only Stone Age weapons. Their task was greatly simplified after they acquired the horse from the Spanish. I learned how the Shoshoni of the high deserts of Nevada used to do it, by talking with Mrs. Kittie Bonner of Austin, who has a trace of Indian blood herself.

"I paint the living memory of Indians," Kittie said. She showed me a painting of a Shoshoni antelope hunt, "just the way it was described to me by Richard Burchin, a Shoshoni friend of mine." Here's what Richard had told her:

"Chief Toy Toy would send out the scouts and let the tribes know there would be a big fandango somewhere along Reese River. The chief set the time and the place, and he would give orders to the scouts: 'Get the young pine-nut tree [piñon] with few berries on top.' They would bring the tree to the fandango ground, and all night they would dance around the tree and chant, and this was for food and for rain and mostly for a good pine-nut crop. Then in a few days, after prayers for a good hunt, the chief would ask the tribe to help corral the antelope for their meat. Then the Indians would go out, four steps apart, and pile up brush to hide behind along a V-shaped place marked by rope made of twisted rabbit fur and sagebrush. When the corral was done, everybody would go out and place themselves behind the brush piles, and this man, on the only horse that was ever known down in the Smith Creek Valley, would drive the antelope toward the corral. Then the Indians would come from behind the brush and keep the antelope going on down into the corral. When the corraling was done, the rider began to slaughter the animals. Their chief was there to divide the food among all his Indians."

Prayers for the hunt, prayers for rain, for marriage, birth, and at death—prayers spoken, sung, and danced pervaded Indian life, along with a feeling of identity with all creation. Pueblo hunters took time to honor their slain animals briefly with coverings of blankets, with precious ornaments of turquoise and shell, letting the creatures lie a little while "in pathetic splendor." Hopis say that "whenever they killed a large wild animal they . . . asked its forgiveness."

I admired the Hopis for their desert farming. On their lofty mesas in northeast Arizona, where rains come seldom and fall haphazardly, they deep-till the sandy soil to tap residual moisture. They shield the tender plants when winds threaten, and channel runoff into a few dike-waffled fields on the upper slopes. I'd read of similar methods employed by prehistoric Indians, and I was pleased to discover that the system was producing plump juicy watermelons today for Indian and Mexican alike on low desert country near Guaymas in southern Sonora.

"When the late summer rains come," Alejandro (Chato) Arias, a Mexican farmer, explained, "the water runs down from those hills to the east. We channel it into our fields, and the dikes trap it. In November we plant the seeds deep, about a foot. Even if no more rains come, they will have enough moisture to grow."

By coincidence I had arrived in April, melon season, and Chato cut into one so burstingly ripe that it opened with a ripping sound at hardly more than the insertion of the knife. While we talked, squatting in his dusty field in the warm sun, he deftly speared a chunk of the heart on his knife blade and served it to me. When shadows grew long we moved to the veranda of his low-roofed adobe house, where I met the rest of the Arias family, smiling wife Alejandra and a stairstep lineup of ten children beginning with 22-year-old Pedro. "You have many mouths to feed," I said to him a bit later. "Is farming enough?"

"We get by," Chato said. "Sometimes we go out and find a tortoise. Other times we have javelina, or doves, or pigeons, sometimes quail. We use many wild plants, and we pick the saguaro fruit and eat it fresh or make it into preserves. We cook the flesh of the barrel cactus with sugar on it and make candy."

From food gatherer to dry farmer to master of irrigation, that was the evolution over thousands of years that produced the desert's highest Indian cultures. I remember the excitement I felt a few years ago when I first realized the scale of Pueblo Bonito in New Mexico's Chaco Canyon—a vast half-moon of an apartment building big enough to shelter a thousand people. It stood as high as four stories and enclosed 650 rooms. The pueblo's stonework was skilled and neat, showing the patience of the Anasazi, or Ancient Ones—a people building for the ages. Farming methods similar to Chato's and the Hopis' made it all possible, producing good crops of corn, beans, and squash so the Indians could lead a settled life.

Then I heard of a prehistoric city of the Chichimecan Indians in Chihuahua that was in some ways even more impressive—in power and trading importance; in number of estimated inhabitants, about 5,000; in extent, about 90 acres. Appropriately it is called Casas Grandes—Big Houses. To get there I drove 120 arid miles south from the New Mexico border. The road ribboned over ridges that darkened to purple with distance, along wide dry valleys, with few ranches or towns to be seen. But Nuevo Casas Grandes, near the ruin site, was a metropolis of many thousands, and included a sprinkling of neat red brick homes built by Mormons who emigrated from the United States late in the 19th century.

In contrast to today's town, the ancient one seemed dead indeed. But even so, its maze of thick clay walls, some still towering three stories or more, excited wonder. And I had the words of Dr. Charles C. Di Peso to bring the town alive. About 15 years ago he led an expedition of his Amerind Foundation of Dragoon, Arizona, in the most extensive excavation of the site ever undertaken—about 37 acres. "Casas Grandes had running water, temples, and ball courts," he said. "Grand colonnades lined galleries and impressive doorways looked out on broad patios. Merchants grew rich dealing in shells from the Pacific, turquoise, salt, peyote, and

Overleaf: *Navajo matrons in a hogan in New Mexico spin wool for rugs they will weave on hand looms and sell at trading posts. Descendants of warlike nomads who migrated from Canada about 1500, Navajos live primarily as farmers and herders in the Southwest.*

ADAM WOOLFITT

slaves. Coppersmiths and jewelers became artists, and a strong priest caste arose."

On one of the raised platforms, where perhaps feather-decked priests once danced, I looked westward to the hills; there faint signs of the complex of channels that once irrigated the valley are still visible.

Of course the real irrigationists settled nearly 2,300 years ago in the broad Salt and Gila River Valleys of Arizona. They were the Hohokam—a Pima word for "those that have vanished." Modern man only in the last few decades has begun to appreciate what the Hohokam accomplished, for they left few obvious clues.

"They cremated their dead," Dr. Emil W. Haury of the University of Arizona told me. "For some reason we seldom find any of the clay figurines or the earthen vessels they made, some in human form, that haven't been smashed. Few signs of their structures survive. Wind and water have blanketed their irrigation works, which we have learned to uncover again through careful excavation."

In 1964-5 Dr. Haury led an extensive excavation of a Gila River site called Snaketown and made an amazing discovery. "The Hohokam had built three miles of irrigation canals as early as 300 B.C.," he said. But he cautions us not to credit them as pioneers in the art; they were people who knew a good thing when they saw it. "They apparently came from the south, where Middle American cultures practiced advanced irrigation in the first millennium B.C."

The Hohokam built perhaps 250 miles of canals, with only stone and wooden tools and without draft animals. They knew some astronomy and had learned a form of acid etching on shell. "But I would say their real accomplishment was in adapting so well to the arid land that they could stay in one place 1,500 years," Dr. Haury said. "They achieved a balance with their environment."

Still, it was a delicate balance, and in all the major Indian cultures there were signs of stress between the 12th and 14th centuries.

"Overpopulation—too many people," Robert H. Lister said of Pueblo Bonito. Dr. Lister, chief of the New Mexico Archeological Center in Albuquerque, cited evidence of hills stripped of timber, increased erosion, deepening arroyos. By 1200 the Anasazi had left Pueblo Bonito forever.

Then came a further woe that spanned the whole region, "something to do with climate," Dr. Haury suspects. Tree-ring studies give us a picture of prolonged drought from 1276 to 1299, and Dr. Di Peso mentioned internal strife, perhaps a revolt, at Casas Grandes. Whatever the cause, healthy cultures declined, and declining ones slumped even further. The great galleries at Casas Grandes became the hovels of the lowly, and the water system was neglected and fell into disrepair. The canals of the Hohokam filled with sand.

I have traveled southeast Utah's Salt Creek Canyon, and spotted ruin after ruin in the space of a few miles. And I climbed one day to a crescent of tumbled structures under a rock overhang and gazed into a kiva, the ceremonial house for men. What had it been like, I wondered, to sit in its cool depth? As I stood there, I suddenly realized that my right index finger was resting in the shallow fingerprint of someone who had helped mortar the kiva wall. It was an electric moment—I'd reached through centuries and touched hands with another human being.

The living past of the Anasazi flows in the veins of present-day Pueblo Indians, and in some of the cultural adaptations of the Navajos. The Pimas and Papagos probably share Hohokam blood. So we went to Taos Pueblo to taste the nutlike

Bold patterns *surround Bill Young, manager of the Hubbell Trading Post on the Navajo Reservation in Arizona. Opened in 1876, the post served Indians who traded silver jewelry and woven goods for such wants as coffee, flour, and tobacco; today it also attracts tourists.*

SAM ABELL

freshness of that loaf of still-warm bread and made small talk about a flawless June day; we went to an arts and crafts center on the Pima reservation and bought a basket; we went to Ganado and Canyon de Chelly to visit Navajoland.

Actually, we were on the edge of historic Navajoland in Santa Fe when we called on Albert H. Schroeder of the National Park Service for a talk about Indian tribal movements. He's a specialist on the subject. "The Navajos and the Apaches are latecomers to the Southwest," he began. "They're Athapascan-speaking peoples, originally from Canada, and they didn't get here until about the 15th or 16th centuries. The Navajos at first settled in northern New Mexico. Then they got into a war with the Utes, who pushed them westward, some as far as northern Arizona. But they still regard the land they first occupied as part of their ancestral home."

No matter how the traveler approaches the Navajo reservation, the land holds drama. From Mexican Hat on the north, the road runs through Monument Valley, among dunes, pinnacles, and lofty mesas; colors shift from moody tans to vibrant reds; vast sweeps of emptiness reach to the horizons. Coming from the south, the visitor passes through the Painted Desert—part of the Great Basin—and Petrified Forest National Park, where trees that stood in the age of dinosaurs now lie fallen amid striped badlands, their trunks turned to agate, sometimes set with amethyst. I came to Ganado on a mild October Saturday and stopped in at the Hubbell Trading Post, where Navajos have been coming to trade since 1876.

"The Navajos have always had pride," post manager Bill Young told me, "pride in their homeland and in the fact that they've been self-supporting."

Arizona pioneer Don Lorenzo Hubbell founded the post and established a reputation with the Indians for fair-dealing in an era marked by scandal. One of his closest friends was a Navajo, Ganado Mucho, for whom he named the place.

Today the post still serves the Indians, but it's been designated a national historic site, and it's run as a nonprofit operation. Navajos come to buy flour and sugar, a wide-brimmed black felt hat, or maybe a new Pendleton blanket. They bring their own weaving to the post to seek buyers. "I recently was able to get $8,000 for a rug that a woman asked me to sell," Mr. Young said. "That's the most we've ever gotten for one."

I raced with the sun to get to Canyon de Chelly before the last red rays faded. Down there, beneath those thousand-foot walls of sandstone, the Navajos had resisted stubbornly before finally yielding to U.S. forces in 1864. It was their first defeat as a nation by the white interlopers. They had ably traded blows with Spanish and Mexican forces over a span of two centuries.

It was in front of a hogan in Canyon de Chelly that a Navajo boy some years ago had drawn his first pictures in the sand. He grew up to become an artist of national reputation, R. C. Gorman. He was born premature and sickly, and was nursed to health on goat's milk and coffee, his grandmother's prescription. He became a man of deep eyes and firm nose and chin, to look like—in his own words—"the Indian on the nickel."

I toured his gallery in Taos, where he exhibits not just his own works but also those of other artists whom he serves as agent. His favorite theme has been Navajo women. In bold but sensitive lines he depicts generous forms, hands accustomed to serving, faces that reflect endurance, prayer, hope.

"Will the Navajo endure?" I asked him. "I don't know, but I'm proud of what they've done so far," he replied. As examples, he cited their rug weaving, sandpainting, and silver work, all artistic skills borrowed from the Spaniards or other Indians and now a source of millions of dollars annually.

Spain's culture lives vigorously over much of the Southwest—in Santa Fe's narrow streets and adobe walls, in Albuquerque's restored Old Town Plaza, in southern Arizona's close economic and social ties with Sonora, in music, place names, and a gracious touch in speech and manner. We found it most strongly in two special places south of the border—Magdalena de Kino in Sonora and San Ignacio in Baja California.

In Magdalena we visited the shrine of an early padre who seemed to exemplify those resolute missionaries of the 17th and 18th centuries. Father Eusebio Francisco Kino founded 27 missions, including the one where gleaming San Xavier del Bac stands today, near Tucson. Through drought, desert heat and cold, time, political intrigue, and frontier Indian uprisings, he remained steadfast in his work.

"His final act as a priest was to bestow a blessing on his people," Dr. Gabriel Sánchez de la Vega told Virginia and me at the shrine that shelters his bones. "He was dedicating a new chapel here in 1711, on this very spot, when he collapsed. That night he died, and he was buried under the floor of the chapel he had been dedicating. Later the chapel was destroyed in an Apache attack. The place where it stood was gradually forgotten as a series of other structures were built."

This century brought renewed interest in the exploits of the pioneer priest, but several attempts to relocate his remains failed. Then an intensified search in 1966 finally revealed the burial site. Now visitors can look down through glass ports to see the bones just as archeologists uncovered them.

Spain's first thrusts into the unknown frontier were fired by quests for gold rather than souls. The treasures of the Aztecs and Incas made all tales of incredible wealth believable. In 1540-42 Francisco Vásquez de Coronado led an expedition up the Rio Grande Valley and as far as the plains of Kansas in search of the Seven Cities of Cíbola, supposedly rich with gold. But the pueblos were of clay and the Indians valued not gold but turquoise. Even so, the Spaniards kept trying for decades. Then the padres took over the lead in extending the frontier, winning souls, building churches, planting fields and vineyards; the civil service and the soldiers came along in the church's wake.

The first Spaniards understood the land, for it was like home. "They tended to come from central Spain, where the terrain and climate and vegetation were very similar," Sid Brinckerhoff, director of the Arizona Historical Society in Tucson, said. "They came from livestock country, and they brought ranching to the Southwest," I had been told in Santa Fe by Fray Angelico Chavez, a historian whose own ancestry goes back to earliest Spanish-colonial times. "Even today you almost always find their descendants raising cattle rather than crops. If they have a choice, they'd rather move to the city and get a job than become farmers."

But if the Spanish understood the land, the Indians on the land were another matter. There was friction here, exploitation there, and recurring strife over long periods before widening common interests brought the mellower times we know today. In a major revolt in 1680, the peaceful Pueblos, with the help of the warlike Apaches and Navajos, drove the Governor, all Spanish colonists, and many of their Indian allies out of northern New Mexico—and kept them out for 12 years. They occupied the Governor's Palace in Santa Fe and built pueblo-style rooms on its roof. Now the rooms have long been removed, and descendants of the Indians come daily to the plaza side of the palace to sell their exquisite handmade wares.

And understanding widens. Hopis dance with live rattlesnakes in their mouths to bring rain, and draw appreciative attention rather than scornful bigotry. Spaniards, Indians, and a mixture of the two mingle at the carnivals that precede Lent. The timeless aura of the 19th century seems to linger in isolated Mexican towns, especially in Baja California. We found such a town in San Ignacio.

San Ignacio has water, springs of it that flow night and day into a lagoon, into networks of ditches that sluice it away to the courtyards and patios of the town, that wind it sparkling among thousands of date palms, to the roots of thousands of grape vines, to orange and lemon trees, to drinking troughs for cattle. San Ignacio is an oasis in a desert land, and for almost 250 years it has gladdened the hearts of those who crossed the desert to get there.

Only about 1,200 souls live in San Ignacio—and life flows easily and unhurried. Barking dogs, not sirens, sound the night's small alarms, and roosters crow the town awake. This has been the order of things since black-robed Jesuits discovered the springs and founded a mission in 1728. A church, built by the Dominicans in 1786, still stands on the plaza, its weathered stone bell tower silhouetted against the sky. Sadly, disease took a devastating toll of the Indians the missionaries had come to save, and none worship there today, though the church still serves the town.

The closer we got to San Ignacio, the more times we were advised, "Be sure to meet Becky Carillo." Soon we were knocking on the front door of her stucco-faced one-story house, on a narrow street a block north of the plaza.

"I'm sorry, my only room for overnight guests is already filled," Becky said, "but you're welcome to use the yard."

So we wheeled our Travelall through her back gate, and unrolled sleeping bags in the rear, as we had done many nights. We slept well but not late. Becky's backyard wakes early: roosters and a clucking hen with chicks, and cats, dogs, and birds. And quite a few people. We were parked near the outdoor convenience and so met the household while awaiting our turn. At breakfast there were other introductions—to the doctor, schoolteacher, an aunt of Becky's, and various friends. Through it all Becky, who neither looks nor acts her 72 years, served eggs cooked ranchero style, with hot sauce, or fried sunny-side up as requested, and managed to talk with everyone, in Spanish or English as required.

She said she returned to San Ignacio a few years ago after decades in the States, where she had married, raised a family, lost a husband, and worked as a translator. She had come back to take care of her mother, who had turned 100 not long before. We asked her about the huge grape arbor in her yard. "We know that those vines are more than a hundred years old," she said, "because they were already large when my mother was brought here as a child of 2. They're from cuttings planted by the first padres. We call them mission grapes. They resemble Concords, but not so many in a cluster, and they're sweet right off the vine."

That evening she offered us each a glass of mission wine. It had a deep red color and tasted pleasantly sweet, with just a hint of salt. We sipped it while sitting near the arbor, where clear water ran in a narrow, curving channel. The ditch was part of a network begun by the early missionaries to distribute San Ignacio's spring water to every piece of property.

With the wine lingering on our tongues, we strolled through town, trying the benches under the huge green Indian laurel trees on the plaza, admiring the roofs paved with drying peppers, peering into little stores to see their wares, for most had no signs on the outside. Occasionally a local truck passed along the narrow streets. A few tourist cars rattled in, covered with dust from the rough, punishing road. Soon all the vehicles seemed to get settled for the night, as did the people.

We strolled back to Becky's and prepared to retire to a real bed, for we had the only overnight room this time. We weren't quite quick enough for the town generator, which shut down at 9:30, but there were kerosene lamps for night owls. As I lay down, I remembered the taste of the mission wine. It was, I thought, a pleasant way to get a taste of history.

"White Dove of the Desert," the mission of San Xavier del Bac near Tucson, Arizona, gleams under a full moon just minutes before sunset. The original structure, built about 1700 by Father Eusebio Francisco Kino, a Jesuit missionary and explorer, burned in 1768; Franciscan priests completed the present church in 1797. A devout and tireless missionary, Father Kino ventured as far as Baja California, established a string of 27 missions in Arizona and Sonora, and converted thousands of Indians to his faith. At the same time, he introduced cattle ranching and sugarcane as well as new fruits, vegetables, and grains to the tribes he worked among. In 1711 he suffered a fatal collapse while bestowing a blessing on a chapel filled with his followers.

First grade *Papago Indian children pray with an Apache nun during Mass in the west chapel of San Xavier del Bac. Besides ministering to the Papagos' reservation, the mission provides a school for Indian children. Father Kino named the mission for his patron, St. Francis Xavier — a 16th-century priest and one of the original Jesuits. Prayers to St. Xavier, said Father Kino, once saved him from a grave illness.*

Rude cross *in hand, St. Francis Xavier points heavenward from the altar of a mission named for him in Baja California. Of 30 churches established on the peninsula by 1834, this structure near Loreto and one other, at La Paz, remain intact. Spanish missionaries, though faced by harsh terrain and often hostile Indians, determinedly spread the tenets of their faith across much of the country's desert lands.*

SAM ABELL

Exuberant riders *charge and retreat in front of the crumbling Hacienda Santiago, once a home of Don Luis Terrazas, a powerful landowner and politician in Chihuahua. A forceful, haughty man, he controlled seven million acres and the lives of thousands of peasant farmers. But in 1910 revolutionaries such as Pancho Villa overran his empire and forced him to flee to the United States. Terrazas died in 1923 at the age of 94 — only months after returning home from exile. Above, grizzled Tomás Acosta, 67, caretaker of the 70-year-old hacienda, stands under a portico with his wife. He recounts that Terrazas, once asked if he came from Chihuahua, arrogantly replied, "I AM Chihuahua."*

SAM ABELL (BELOW)

Reed-thatched roof shelters 18-year-old Maria Luna and one of her two children in their adobe house in Boquillas del Carmen, a Mexican village of about 125 people who earn their living as feldspar miners in the desolate country across the Rio Grande from Big Bend National Park, Texas. Attentive Boquillas pupils listen to their teacher (above); some 30 children attend the town's two-room, four-grade school.

Bed and fireplace share a kitchen wall at Las Golondrinas, a ranch near Santa Fe, New Mexico. Reconstructed by its owner in the Spanish style of the 18th and 19th centuries, the ranch complex includes houses, outbuildings, watermills, and a country store.

The Miracle of Moisture

SUMMER THUNDERHEADS took ever bigger bites out of the Utah sunset. Boiling black clouds curtained off the afterglow, and gusts whiplashed the campfire where we clustered—my family and friend Ted Ekker, our guide in this southeast corner of his native state. "These desert storms blow by quickly," Ted forecast. "Even when you think thunder and lightning are going to tear up the world, the clouds move on after a few drops."

The lightning was horrendous. Multi-armed bolts jabbed heaven and earth. Staccato flashes conjured darkness into day, alternating blackout with bright images of orange cliffs. Volleys of thunder bounced off the high sandstone walls around us with an unremitting roar that shook the soles of our feet.

The first few drops kicked up a dusty smell, almost stopped, and then gradually multiplied to soaker status. We huddled under our ponchos and admired how well our fire burned even in a downpour—until suddenly it went out with a steamy hiss. What the raindrops had not managed to do upon descent, they achieved on the ground; they collected into a two-inch sheet that flowed down the slope where we stood and drowned the fire's underlying bed of embers.

Now the storm approached gully-washer stage; water surged downhill, rushing over the hard-baked earth and rock-mantled cliffs. Runoff cascaded into sandy washes and stream beds, usually bone-dry. Ted spoke of some gully washers he had seen, flash floods with walls of water five or six feet high that swept away cattle and turned cowboys aquatic. He remembered a crossing on Utah's Dirty Devil river so altered in a single rainy season that a horse and wagon almost sank from sight in the mud where once the bottom had been solid. I also recalled stories I had read of people carried to their deaths in desert floods, three in the Death Valley area alone during the wet winter of 1969. Signs at low places along western highways warn motorists: "Watch Out for Flash Floods."

After a couple of hours the storm moved on east, and we got some sleep under a starry sky that appeared more brilliant for its recent washing. The sun came up white gold in a turquoise sky.

On many other evenings we watched lightning-barbed pillars of cloud sweep from horizon to horizon without getting us wet. We hiked in powdery dust where no rain had fallen for months. But even there we found ripple marks in rocks and on sand, and flood-gouged arroyos, as these dry waterways are called. These seams

Sky-splitting bolt of lightning, signaling a cloudburst, strikes the Chisos Mountains in Big Bend National Park, Texas. Storm clouds often pass over the thirsty desert regions without bestowing a drop of water, and months without rain may separate rare downpours.

PHLOX DIFFUSA (UPPER); NATIONAL GEOGRAPHIC PHOTOGRAPHER JAMES L. STANFIELD

and scars, the signatures that violent floodwater writes on the land all over desert country, have prompted the description: "The pipes are installed, but somebody forgot to turn on the water."

As Ted's rancher brother Arthur Ekker told me: "If you have water, you have everything. If you don't have water, you have nothing."

Art spoke out of many years of experience. He has grazing rights to 400 square miles of rangeland, and its capacity is figured at about one cow per square mile. The problem is water. In good years the blue grama and Indian rice grass grow thick and luscious, and the herds can choose between a dozen or so springs, ponds, or watering tanks. In bad years the range withers early or never sprouts, and only three far-flung springs can be depended upon to flow. "Title to the land in this old desert isn't worth the paper it's written on unless you've got the water rights to go with it," Art added.

In simplest terms, the deserts are where water isn't—or almost isn't. The skin-flint desert sky rations rainfall to about eight inches a year. But even this is just a statistical average. Yuma, Arizona, for example, may receive half its annual total of three inches in one or two fierce summer cloudbursts. This total also varies from year to year. Places in the Mojave may get less than an inch one year and receive as much as 12 the next.

Little rain, uneven distribution, rapid evaporation, soil too porous to hold moisture or too packed to accept it—these are some of the conditions that earn a land its desert label. But why are our deserts where they are?

By stealing moisture from the air, mountains create deserts. When the moist winds from the Pacific hit the California and Oregon ranges, they climb upward to clear the mountain wall in their path. As the mountains force the air to rise, it cools, and the moisture condenses and falls as rain or snow on the western, windward slopes. Then, drained of much of their moisture, these same westerlies descend the leeward side. The air, compressed and heated in its downward slide, brings winds that blow thirsty and warm across the Great Basin and northern parts of the other American deserts. These are the lands left dry because they lie in the rain shadow of the western mountains.

The pattern of air circulation around the globe also keeps things arid farther south. High, large-scale air currents send cool, dry air from aloft to the earth below. Sailors traditionally call these regions of calm and little rain the horse latitudes. On land this fair-weather zone, with its descending dry air, spawns the desert.

And so the blessing of rain, accepted so casually in moist regions, can be cause for celebration in desert country. On the sun-bleached mesas of the Hopi Reservation and in the Pueblo world along the Rio Grande, Indians still dance in ritual prayers for rain. Gourd rattles imitate the patter of raindrops; bull-roarers—wooden slats tied to the ends of thongs—swing with the sound of thunder; feathers and tufts of eagle down carry the plea to the sky bird, water serpent, and sky gods.

To see rain approach and then miss your wilting corn patch by half a mile is agony. To see curtains of water falling straight down at you but never reaching the earth is a special kind of torture that desert people know. In any climate the air will absorb some rain on the way down, but superdry desert air burns it away; earth-bound creatures can only look up and thirst for the phantom rain.

Muddy runoff *from a storm cascades upon a young adventurer in Arizona's Rider Canyon. Such deluges may cause flash floods that send walls of water rushing down desert arroyos.*

Overleaf: *Hurtling down the roiling Colorado River in the Grand Canyon, passengers and crew in a rubber raft fight a raging current during a National Geographic expedition in 1969.*

What the heavens withhold, the earth supplies to favored regions where the land lies along the few dependable desert rivers, where springs emerge, or where man has trapped surface runoff or tapped subterranean supplies.

Two great rivers—the 1,360-mile Colorado and the 1,885-mile Rio Grande—sustain bountiful life along much of their courses, but man has so tamed their waters that he literally turns them off and on to meet the needs of farms, cities, and factories.

I told James Kirby one morning that I'd like to see the effect of irrigation on the Rio Grande. Jim is a Rio Grande Project Superintendent in El Paso, Texas, for the U. S. Bureau of Reclamation, and it's his job to know the river. I got into Jim's car, and we drove southeast down the broad river valley, which spread green and fruitful as far as the irrigation water went. The line between greenery and sand was often so distinct that you could stand with one foot in a verdant field of alfalfa and the other on parched desert.

We drove through fields of cotton, chili, alfalfa, and onions, past machine shops and tractor sheds of huge farms, through little towns with adobe houses and churches that recalled the days of Spanish friars and Mexican vaqueros.

At last we parked by a diversion dam across the river itself. On a walkway atop the dam I looked downstream, and, except for a solitary puddle here and there, I saw an empty stream bed stretching out of view.

"There's no appreciable flow for about 290 miles," Jim said, "until the Rio Conchos in Mexico and other tributaries flow in." The river at this point had been totally diverted into a system of canals, and the river bed itself was dry. Dust devils whirled upon its sandy surface.

Across the arid West, men like Jim Kirby master the desert by diverting streams into irrigation canals and storing water behind dams. Thus they control the irregular flow of rivers and convert desolate lands into lush oases.

Of the Arizona Territory J. Ross Browne, adventurer and author, wrote in 1864: "With millions of acres of the finest arable lands there was not . . . a single farm under cultivation." By 1911, the Roosevelt Dam and a system of canals had reclaimed the Salt River Valley, and irrigated fields yielded crops the year round.

The miracle of moisture makes apricots and melons ripen, grapes fill out, and cotton explode into fluffy, white bolls. Dams parcel out water to the valleys of the Verde, the Gila, the Green, the San Juan, and to southern California's Imperial Valley—the Nation's winter salad bowl.

"Crops don't fail when farmers can pick up a phone and ask for water," says Rollie Clark, one of the pioneers in the valley. All its water comes through the All-American Canal—an 80-mile trough across the Sonoran Desert. The canal, diverting about a fourth of the flow of the Colorado River, has made farmers in the valley forget about drought. But Rollie Clark, who came to the valley in a covered wagon in 1902, remembers harder times.

"Forty acres of canteloupes washed away when the Colorado went on a rampage in 1905. Then during the drought of '34 the river dried up, and we drove to El Centro every week for our 20-gallon ration of drinking water," he recalls. "A truck came by with water for our cows and hogs, but we lost $10,000 that year when our crop of kafir corn failed."

Before the Hoover Dam backed the Colorado up to create Lake Mead, a 115-mile-long boatman's paradise in the blistering desert on the Arizona-Nevada border, the river either nearly ran dry or overflowed its banks and flooded the valley.

"In the old days we drew our drinking water from irrigation ditches into a 50-gallon tank. We let it settle overnight, and by morning we had 30 gallons of water and 20 gallons of mud," Rollie adds. Today three desilting basins clear Colorado water where it is diverted into the canal, but nothing rids the river of its salt.

Rivers which flow through arid lands pick up mineral salts from the soil. Without rain enough to wash it sweet, desert soil becomes naturally loaded with salt. Then, when these rivers are tapped for irrigation, with their waters being used over and over again, downstream waters grow even saltier.

"Irrigation in the upper Colorado River Basin has more than doubled the salt concentration," said Myron B. Holburt, chief engineer of the Colorado River Board of California.

Soil poisoned with salt has plagued desert agriculture since the dawn of history. The 20th-century answer to the problem lay buried beneath my feet. Long tile pipes six feet below the field drain the salt-laden irrigation water and empty it into ditches instead of letting it evaporate and build up its lethal residue.

Sometimes these salts or alkali encrust great stretches of desert in shimmering, white flats. These playas, as they are called, are dry lakes or brackish, shallow ponds where water has evaporated for centuries. When the sun dries and bakes the playas, they become smooth pavements that extend many miles. That's why addicts of speed on wheels head for the Bonneville Salt Flats on the west edge of the Great Salt Lake Desert in Utah. There Gary Gabelich, racing car driver, pushed his rocket car almost to the sound barrier, reaching 622 miles an hour on a ten-mile track as level as a billiard table.

We wanted to skim over the salt flats too, and so in Wendover we unhitched our trailer and headed for the salt.

Disappointment. The next day would mark the start of the annual Bonneville Nationals—speed trials for a great array of souped-up stock vehicles—and the course was closed for the preparations. Returning to Wendover, I looked speculatively at the flat salt beside the road. It looked solid, and I started to swing onto it when I caught sight of a Mustang ahead, mired to the hubs. The water table here was right at the surface; the salt was supersaturated and like putty under a thin crust. The Mustang driver was too far from the pavement for our chain to reach, so we helped him get a tow truck to the scene.

The reason for all that water under salt is simple. The Great Salt Lake Desert is a drainage basin for all the blue mountains that ring it, and many that lie beyond. And while there's little rain to drain off, what little there is collects in the basin, making much of the salt treacherous. Great Salt Lake itself, the shrinking remnant of an inland sea, suffers tremendous losses by evaporation. Result: the lake is as much as eight times saltier than the sea. Evaporation takes a toll of all desert waters; Lake Mead loses more than 250 billion gallons a year.

Water in Nature's underground reservoirs doesn't evaporate, but it too is declining. Man is beginning to pump these ground-water basins dry. Two-thirds of the water used in Arizona comes from the ground. "Even if we didn't have a rainfall in five years, no one would have to turn off the tap," explains H. M. Babcock of the United States Geological Survey in Tucson. But, like many others, he knows the water shortage will catch up with them soon enough, and depletion is a widening worry. As the supply of ground water dwindles, pumping costs rise and valley floors sink as the dewatered land shrinks. Somewhere ahead looms disaster unless use and supply can be balanced.

Deeper wells, more dams, longer aqueducts have, according to Walter Prescott Webb, historian of the West, created an oasis civilization in the desert, where people have water in abundance. Now man with his incredible technology and his increasing numbers has the power to mine water away. And water is the very key to life, especially in the desert.

Snow whitens the banks of a reservoir on the Williams & Sons Guest Ranch near Pioche, Nevada. Wintering at the pond, mallard ducks swim on a November morning; falling snow powders last summer's weeds, standing brittle in the cold. The reservoir, fed by a permanent spring, offers swimming in summer and ice skating in winter.

SAM ABELL

Under way *at sunrise, fishermen in a small skiff trail a wake that creases the desert-rimmed Gulf of California. Breeding area for many ocean fish, the gulf for centuries supplied Indians with food. Today, its waters attract thousands of commercial and sport fishermen.*

Bounty *of the Gulf of California litters the deck of the shrimp boat Salvación as the crew sorts and cleans the catch off Baja California. Pelicans and other seabirds follow the boat to snatch discarded bits of shrimp and small fish snagged in the nets. The gulf, formed several million years ago after vast earthquakes split the Baja peninsula away from mainland Mexico, plunges to a depth of more than two miles in places.*

Sand dunes border the All-American Canal west of Yuma, Arizona. Fed by impounded Colorado River water, the wide trough stretches west 80 miles through desert to southern California's lush Imperial Valley. There the waters irrigate more than half a million acres, bringing forth year-round crops of vegetables, fruit, cotton, and cattle feed. Although irrigation gradually concentrates natural salts in the soil and eventually can make it sterile, farmers in the Imperial Valley combat this process through selective planting, fertilization, and special drainage techniques.

Biplane sprays insecticide on pecan groves at Stahmann Farms near Las Cruces, New Mexico—one of the world's largest pecan acreages. Water from the nearby Rio Grande irrigates some 180,000 trees thriving where scrub mesquite once grew. The Stahmann family first planted and watered seedlings in 1933.

Meandering canal in Baja California carries Colorado River water into irrigated fields of vegetables. Such canals empty the Colorado of most of its water before it reaches the Gulf of California.

Huge plumes of dust, lifted from the floor of Owens Valley in California, ride skyward on the Sierra Wave. Dry westerly winds, robbed of moisture as they crossed over the lofty Sierra Nevada, now hurtle down the eastern slopes with the force of

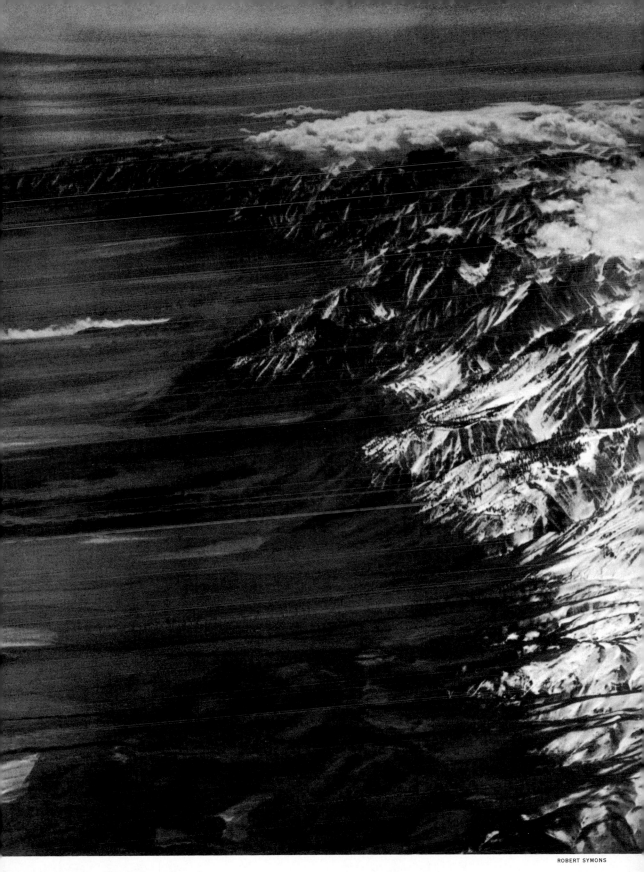

a hurricane. They billow the valley air
upward as much as 8,000 feet a minute to
heights approaching ten miles.

Evaporation ponds *mirror cotton-ball clouds floating above the Wasatch Range and eastern shore of Utah's Great Salt Lake. Canals of the Great Salt Lake* *Minerals & Chemicals Corporation carry lake brine to shallow ponds that cover 14,000 acres; evaporation leaves a harvest of common salt and compounds*

of potassium, sodium, magnesium, and other minerals. Different colors indicate varying brine concentrations as minerals settle out of the solutions.

Desert pupfish at the Arizona-Sonora Desert Museum near Tucson drift among Vallisnaria, a common aquarium plant. These blue Cyprinodon macularius males measure $2\frac{1}{2}$ inches. Pupfish normally live in isolated springs and pools in the Southwest; some species occur only in a single pond.

Dripping rows of porous pipes (top) supply fresh water to collecting troughs at an experimental desalinization plant in Roswell, New Mexico. In the desalting process, pumps force brine into the pipes under pressure. Thin plastic membranes within the pipes filter out the salt.

Swimmers riding air mattresses and inner tubes crowd Big Surf, a resort with an artificial lagoon near Phoenix, Arizona. Water suddenly released from a reservoir—as much as 90,000 gallons at a time—surges toward the beach in waves as high as five feet. Above, a surfer more than 150 miles from the nearest ocean tumbles from his board, wiped out by a breaker.

Water, Wind, And Cataclysm Shape the Land

AT THE GRAND CANYON'S RIM, the world ends precipitously. We could see where it begins again—eight miles straight ahead, or a mile down. Not far away, ravens wheeled in the summer-heated air, their huge, diffused shadows playing giant leapfrog on buttes and terraces at least half a mile below. We stood at Cape Royal on the North Rim, and tried to grasp the canyon's size.

"Daddy, has the river stopped?" asked seven-year-old John. He pointed to distant Unkar Rapid. Its minuscule welts of foam appeared fixed, its motion frozen. But as the day waned, the rock faces looming above the river seemed to be moving, made higher by deepening shadows and the play of the sunset's fiery pinks and oranges and rich lavenders.

In 1869 one-armed Maj. John Wesley Powell led the first authenticated descent of the Colorado River, and paused awestruck "in the depths of the earth." Then he described his feelings as he gazed at the sheer walls and cliffs soaring to the world above: "... the great river shrinks into insignificance ... the waves are but puny ripples, and we but pigmies, running up and down the sands. . . ."

Less than pygmies. Ants perhaps, I thought. Early next day, to gain a better sense of the canyon's vastness, we got on mules and rode down a bit of the North Kaibab Trail. It clings to an almost vertical wall that, top to bottom, reveals about two billion years of earth history. Erosion has erased the last 150 million years, but two other water-carved features in the region, Zion Canyon and the amphitheater of Bryce Canyon National Park, retain those more recent strata. Combined, the three places offer glimpses of just about all the major geologic eras.

Aside from its revelation of earth history, the Grand Canyon drew me because much of it is vertical desert in a 217-mile-long gash through a fairly well-watered plateau. At the canyon bottom grow barrel cactus and mesquite, and in summer the heat sometimes rivals Death Valley's; near the top, sagebrush gradually gives way to piñon pine, juniper, and oak; finally, on the plateau, stand forests of ponderosa pine, interspersed on the North Rim with spruce, fir, and aspen.

As we descended into the canyon, the ponderosa pine and aspen vanished above a battlemented cliff of buff sandstone that once was shifting desert dunes. The cliff receded ever higher into the north sky's deep blue, and the August sun turned suddenly hot as we switchbacked through a 300-foot-thick layer of Hermit Shale, once the floodplain of ancient rivers which (Continued on page 74)

Reaching for a toehold on a wall of rock, a climber tests his skill in Lower Granite Gorge near the western end of the Grand Canyon. Here ten million years of cutting and polishing by the Colorado River have exposed this 1.7-billion-year-old Vishnu schist—the canyon's bedrock.

DWARF BUCKWHEAT (ERIOGONUM OVALIFOLIUM) UPPER

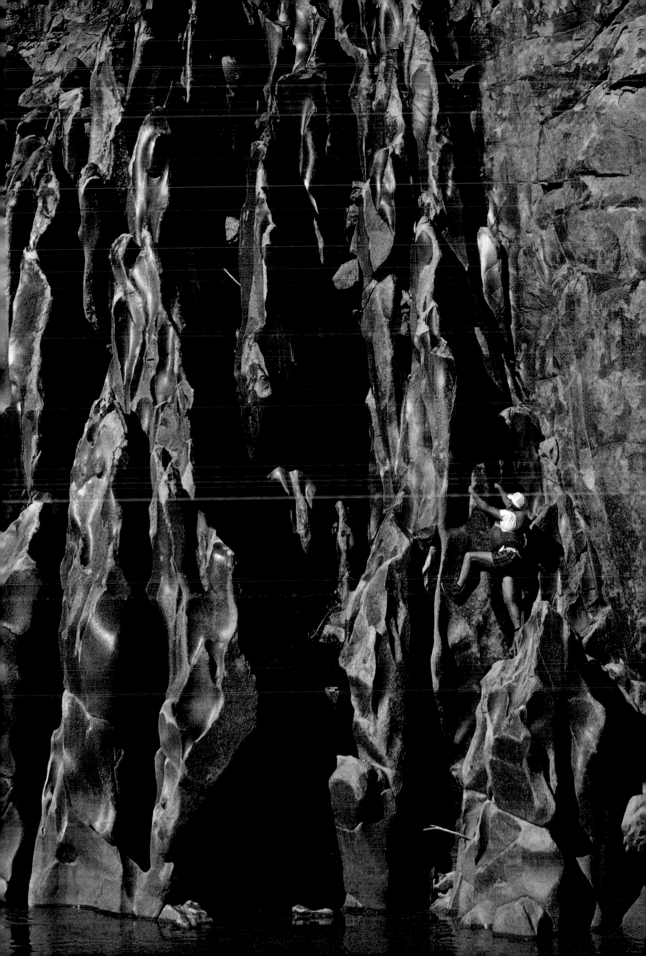

Lighted collage, *made in part of polished slabs of translucent agate, glows in the shop of rock hound Dr. John Dale Owen at Cave Creek, Arizona. He holds a crystal-encrusted piece of barite.*

Weekend prospector *E. W. Darrah chips at a 500-million-year-old limestone boulder, seeking fossil trilobites in Ike's Canyon, Nevada. A sudden blizzard ended the day's search.*

Petrified log *shadowed by Bigelow asters displays vivid colors from quartz and particles of iron and manganese in Petrified Forest National Park, Arizona. Silica-laden water seeping through the wood eventually replaced each cell with stone. Thousands of such logs lie scattered over the park's 94,189 acres.*

meandered across the desert areas. Mule train boss Stan Stockton stopped us where the trail became a narrow ledge cut back into a sheer wall. "Rock wasps have been a nuisance here this year," he said, "and once in a while they will spook a mule. We haven't lost a rider yet, and we want to keep it that way. So hang on to your saddles." We didn't need cautioning. The canyon had a dizzying grandeur, and we often found ourselves leaning heavily away from the void at the trail's edge.

To a student, geology may be no more than words in a textbook. But here at the Grand Canyon it's a textbook come to life, as it is all over the desert Southwest. This vast region is a complex of canyons and mesas, buttes and spires, arches and natural bridges, mountains formed by great blocks of the earth's surface that have been uplifted or warped or folded, other mountains that ripped away their tops in great volcanic explosions, vast fiery rivers of lava that hardened into black stone, sand in endless transition from rock to dunes and stream beds and back to rock again.

"But what's the difference between a mesa and a butte?" son Steve wanted to know. I'd been using the terms casually as we flew northeastward over the great canyon systems of the Colorado one day: "There's Junction Butte, just north of the confluence of the Colorado and the Green, and north of the butte is a mesa called Island in the Sky."

Well, a mesa—from Spanish for table—stands high, broad, and flat-topped; a butte sometimes looks like a narrower mesa, but the name has been given to many steep, isolated hills and knobs whether flat-topped or not.

Angular mesas, buttes, and spires form the profiles of such memorable landmarks as Monument Valley, which straddles the Arizona-Utah border on the Navajo Reservation, and account in part for the cubist look of vast areas of desert country, including virtually all of the Colorado Plateau and much of New Mexico.

I asked a friend of mine, Dr. William Lee Stokes, University of Utah geologist, what it takes to form a mesa or a butte. "A hard layer, such as lava or sedimentary rock," he replied, "that will remain as a durable cap while water erosion gradually carries away surrounding material. A classic example is Colorado's Grand Mesa. A 100-square-mile lava field forms its top, making it the greatest lava-capped mesa in the West. Of course, the size of any mesa or butte gradually diminishes as erosion undercuts the rimrock and chunks of it fall away.

"To understand these forms, it is as important to keep in mind what has eroded away as it is to know what remains," Dr. Stokes said. "Both mesas and buttes are remnants of continuous layers being removed by erosion. These remnants evolved from plateaus to benches and terraces, then to mesas and buttes. Some of the buttes have eroded and crumbled until only spires remain. Eventually the spires fall, usually piece by piece. Finally the fragments weather into pebbles, and the pebbles weather into sand."

We'd had some experience with falling rock. In Utah's Ticaboo Canyon by Lake Powell we'd camped on a golden summer evening when the loudest sounds were the popping and crackling of our cookfire. Suddenly an explosive thud jarred the stillness and reverberated like a cannon burst. "What was that?" I asked Ted Ekker of Green River, our boatman and guide. "A ledge just fell somewhere," he said.

In great degree, most desert shapes are explained by what has fallen, blown, or washed away. I like the way Dr. Stokes describes the creation of the vast canyon complex that imprisons the Colorado River: "The effects of the river reach far out from the river itself, for the master stream determines the depth and extent of erosion in all the side canyons, down to the smallest arroyos that drain the highest mesas. When rains come, the water gathered into these canyons acquires accelerated energy as it plunges down steep slopes and over precipices, picking up sand and rock. The whole complex, working together, is a great energy machine grinding out an ever-deeper master canyon. And, of course, as the master canyon deepens and widens so do all the side canyons. In this way the Grand Canyon system grows infinitesimally larger with every rain."

But what energies could possibly carve such desert formations as natural bridges and arches? And, for that matter, how do you tell one from the other?

Bates Wilson, just retired as superintendent of three preserves—Arches National Park, Natural Bridges National Monument, and Canyonlands National Park —has been asked that question so many times that he has refined his reply to a single sentence: "A natural bridge spans a watercourse and an arch does not."

That answer also explains how natural bridges are formed, because a stream in time could carve one. But arches? "The answer to that goes back to when this red sandstone lay deep in the earth," said Bates. "Great pressures from below created vertical cracks about every 20 feet or so. Through millions of years, erosion uncovered the sandstone, exposing the cracks. As frost and water penetrated, breaking and washing away rock, the spaces widened between thinning adjacent slabs, or fins. Water and wind beat on their surfaces, eventually making holes in the thinner slabs and gradually enlarging them to form arches."

Arches National Park contains scores of the curious formations, and no one knows how many hundred cast their half-doughnut shadows on the whole Four Corners area, where Utah, Colorado, Arizona, and New Mexico meet. One young man is counting them as a hobby. Dick Wilson of Moab, no kin of Bates, has photographed, measured, or otherwise catalogued 56 in Arches, nearly as many in Canyonlands National Park, and estimates he'll find 200 more worth photographing in the area from Natural Bridges National Monument through the Grand Canyon.

"That includes still another type of formation, the potty arch," he said. "That's when a pothole on top of a cliff erodes down through to a deep recess in the cliff, leaving a hole. The classic example is Paul Bunyan's Potty in Canyonlands Park." I'd seen it—a huge oval skylight perhaps 60 feet across in a vast alcove that shelters ruined cliff homes of the Anasazi.

The rock country's alcoves and ledges offer snug retreats against the weather, and I often placed my sleeping bag under some handy roof of stone. Lee Stokes half-jokingly questioned my wisdom in so doing one night during a Green River cruise we shared. "That shelf you're under is a soft formation called Chinle," he told me, "and it breaks off easily." Nowadays I remember his words when I'm in desert country, and carefully examine overhangs before using them for shelter.

The terms for geologic formations are names to learn the land by. For instance, I connected the Chinle with the Painted Desert and Petrified Forest in northern Arizona. The same formation has surfaced there as a striped badland littered with great stone logs. I'd visited the Petrified Forest as a boy and walked the stone trunks —some, though broken into sections, extended 160 feet—as if I were crossing a log bridge over a Midwest creek. My imagination wasn't far off at that, for about 180 million years ago huge trees washed down from nearby mountains during floods and piled up in marshes that became the Chinle formation. As deepening sediment buried the trunks, silica-laden waters infiltrated the wood, duplicating its structure cell by cell with such minerals as jasper and agate and amethyst.

One reason for my love of desert country is its many mountain aeries that give you that on-top-of-the-world feeling. They can also show you a lot of country—and geology—at a glance. From the top of 12,003-foot-high Sierra Blanca in southern New Mexico's Sacramento Mountains, we gazed toward the northwest and saw coal-black lava beds ringed by sawtoothed mountains. To the southwest, the blinding dunes of the White Sands National Monument spread across 275 square miles of the Tularosa Basin. Beyond them rose the San Andres Mountains and the vertically fluted crests of the Organ Mountains.

No river carved the 150-mile length of the Tularosa, and none flows there today; this is arid country in the extreme, part of the northernmost tongue of the Chihuahuan Desert. The Tularosa was formed when internal stresses cracked two roughly parallel faults, and the land between them dropped. The German word for ditch—graben— is the name given to such troughs, and they corduroy much of the West, including Death Valley.

From Sierra Blanca we descended to White Sands, spurred by the impatience of our three boys to reach what is surely one of the country's biggest sandpiles.

"Make all the footprints you want," a ranger called out as we wound into the heart of the monument, "but please, no car tracks in the dunes." Footprints last only until the next wind retumbles a few million whispering grains, and then the dunes become clean slates again.

Instead of the usual grains of quartz, the white sands are gypsum, washed down from nearby slopes; the gypsum sand is softer than quartz sand, less abrasive, and feels velvety between your toes. The dunes are no place for keeping your shoes on. Virginia and I joined the boys in sole-skiing down the slopes, some of them 50 feet high, and felt like children again. We reached the bottom in a few great tobogganing strides. "I'm a giant," shouted young John.

As I stood among the dazzling slopes of White Sands monument, I seemed surrounded by an endless sea of dunes, and I pondered the popular image of deserts as vast expanses of sand. Actually, they are largely a mixture of bare rocks, pebbly plains, parched soil, and salt-encrusted flats. Dunes cover only a small percentage of our four major desert areas. Still, there's enough sand around to satisfy anyone who craves a realm of dunes—in Death Valley, in Idaho's Bruneau Dunes, in Utah's Coral Pink Sand Dunes, in Colorado's Great Sand Dunes. The latter stand as high as 700 feet, among the world's biggest, dwarfing the stormiest ocean waves. "Dune-building isn't just a matter of having wind move sand," Lee Stokes had told me. "The wind must have the chance to work unhindered over vast periods of time. It carries the finer dust high and far, but it can't lift the coarser grains nearly as easily. Instead it nudges them about."

And the wind never ceases its work. Nothing in the desert is more transitory than the contour of a dune, for the next breeze will reshape it in some degree. When winds blow fiercely, the dunes go on the march. Anything in their path is sandblasted and often buried. The heaviest, most abrasive sand seldom rises above knee height, and rock formations in sandy areas sometimes are undercut by it. Mushroom Rock in Death Valley, an eight-foot-high, black volcanic remnant on a stemlike pedestal, owes its shape in part to this low-scouring effect.

We had quite a different experience sole-skiing in another part of the desert, on slopes almost as black as the White Sands are white—and we did not take our shoes off. We climbed a thousand-foot cinder pile called Sunset Crater, in the San Francisco Peaks volcanic field near Flagstaff, then bounded back down in ten minutes, a fifth of the time it took me to struggle through the loose cinders to the top. And we all picked up sharp grains in our shoes. "It's good that cinders hurt your feet," David said as he poured a small handful (Continued on page 82)

White fishing boats ride the blue waters of Bahía Concepción on the east coast of Baja California. Nearly land-locked, this 25-mile-long bay extends numerous watery fingers into secluded coves. Shells of marine animals, worn down to minute particles no larger than grains of sand, form dazzling white beaches. On the mountains rimming much of the water, tangled desert plants armed with thorns discourage explora-tion. Today, Bahía Concepción faces rapid change as paved highways increas-ingly open the land to development.

Sandstone spires *called The Needles rise hundreds of feet from the valley floor of Canyonlands National Park in southeastern Utah. Rain sculptured the stone after it became exposed when the surrounding earth slowly collapsed — undermined by subsurface water that had dissolved portions of a subterranean salt deposit as big as Maryland and as much as a mile thick.*

Veinlike channels *trace patterns formed by rain runoff near Titus Canyon in California's Death Valley.*

Sandstone chevrons *mark an arroyo near Mexican Hat, Utah. An inland sea deposited these layers along its shores as sand; the grains became compressed and cemented into rock that was exposed to erosion by gradual uplift.*

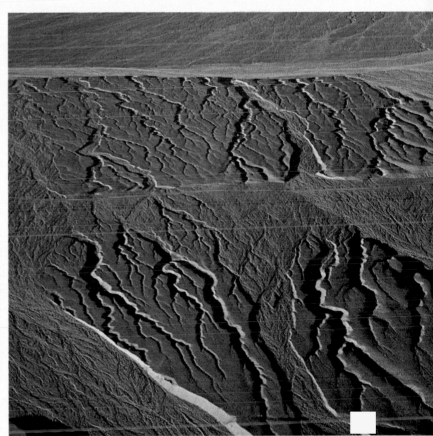

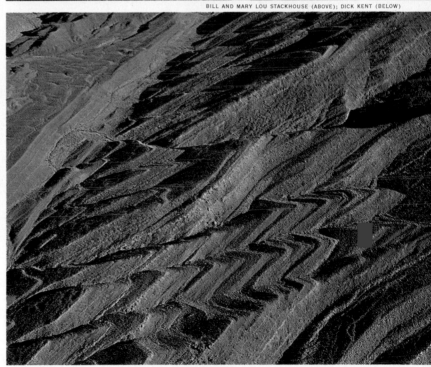

Mute testimonial *to the power of geologic forces, a stone sentinel points skyward from Upheaval Dome in Canyonlands National Park, Utah. Once these tilted strata lay horizontal, about 1,800 feet lower than at present. Then a column of salt pressed upward, forcing the surface rock into a bulging dome. Eventually the crust cracked and eroded into this irregular landscape.*

Famed and feared, *the San Andreas Fault, a fracture in the earth's crust, seams the arid Carrizo Plain northwest of Los Angeles. Earthquakes along the fault result from the horizontal movement of two great sections of the crust called tectonic plates. The continental plate on the left pushes southeast and the Pacific plate on the right pushes northwest. Friction holds the plates together at the surface—and tension builds up—until a sudden slippage repositions them.*

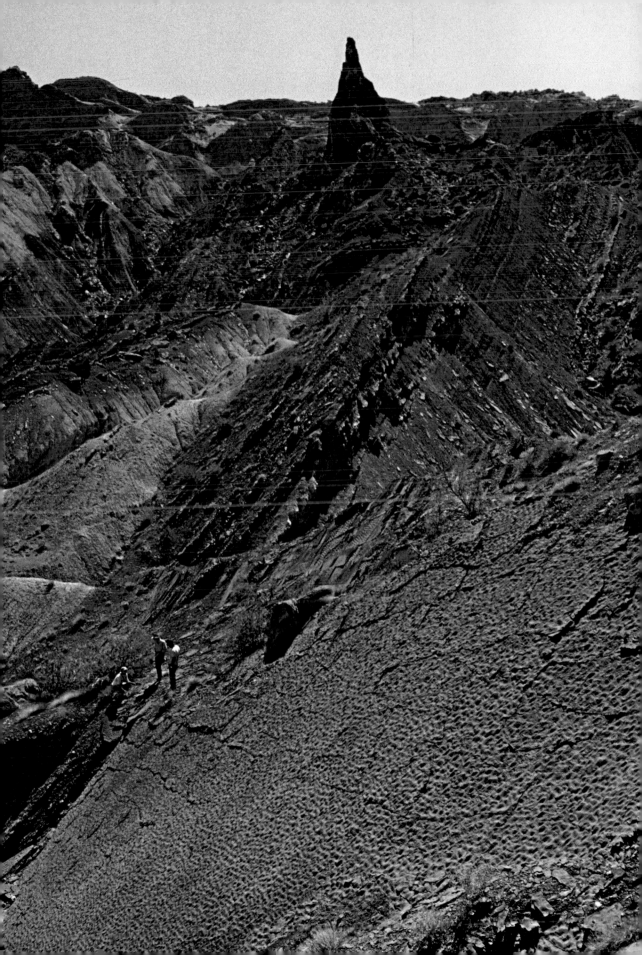

from his shoes. "Otherwise, this place would get carried away a shoeful at a time."

I had especially wanted to look down into Sunset Crater, for from it on a fire-and-brimstone day around 1066 had spewed a vast black cloud that started a land boom over an 800-square-mile area. When the volcano's choking blanket of ash cooled, and new plants poked through the moisture-retaining layer, they showed increased vigor. Indian farmers quickly realized the land had been made more productive, and they moved in from all over the high desert to plant corn and squash in the arroyos, build stone houses, and mingle tribal customs and languages. At nearby Wupatki ruins we saw the remains of what once was a three-story pueblo of brownish red sandstone; it sheltered 300 people and reflected the prosperity of the time. Apparently drought in the 13th century caused them to flee.

"Volcanoes give us material for new rock, in the form of ash and dust and lava flows," Dr. Stokes had told me. "We've talked previously about erosional forms that took land away, and this is the other side of the picture. The Southwest has had much land-building volcanic activity; Sunset Crater erupted a mere 900 years ago."

I had seen the cinder cones and jumbled black lavas of ancient volcanic eruptions from west Texas to California, from Idaho to Baja California. Idaho's Craters of the Moon explain themselves with the name, but I had flown over an area that to me seemed even more lunarlike — the Pinacate volcanic field in northwest Sonora. It is a tortured, lava-encrusted world of ash beds, huge calderas, and cones flanked by high dunes that reach to the head of the Gulf of California. For three years Larry May of Tucson has gone into the forbidding area every few days to gather data for a master's thesis. He estimates the region covers more than 600 square miles, and that one of the largest calderas is 800 feet deep and a mile or so across.

This volcanic field lies close to one of the great earth changers of today, the San Andreas Fault Zone, which cuts northwestward from the head of the Gulf of California along the east side of the Salton Sea, across the Coachella Valley, then on through San Francisco and out into the Pacific. San Andreas is remembered as the fault that suddenly shifted as much as 20 feet in the great earthquake of 1906.

The fault marks the clearly visible shear line between two massive sections of the earth's crust, the continental American plate moving to the southeast, and the Pacific plate moving to the northwest. Though the latter is mostly oceanic, it includes southwest California and all of Baja California. Across southern California's desert country the mismatch of terrain from horizontal slippage along the shear line is unmistakable from the air. Deep-cut arroyos end abruptly at uncreased plains; mountains have lost toes as neatly as if amputated by a surgeon's knife.

Southward this fault zone figures in complex crustal movements that began several million years ago and eventually split the 770-mile-long Baja peninsula away from mainland Mexico. Numerous active faults, tremors and temblors, and signs of recent volcanic activity all label this area one of dynamic geologic change, where new land areas may be rising, in contrast to the erosional forces that wear mountains down.

Desert dryness and heat spread wide, but they don't go deep, and you can prove it by ducking into a limestone cave. We did so at Lehman Caves in eastern Nevada, trading a torrid August sun for the year-round 50° F. moistness of its marbled limestone halls. And at Carlsbad Caverns we dropped down from a 100-degree June day in New Mexico to the constant 56 degrees of a stone fantasyland.

"It's hard to believe we're walking under a desert," Virginia said as she turned up her jacket collar. This was a different world. Our looping path took us through a stunning series of chambers where emerald pools reflected ceiling draperies in stone, where giant stalagmites rose glistening from the floor. In the Big Room, a half-mile long and a thousand feet wide, we beheld a stonescape that surely belonged to another planet—forests of spikes and knobs and rippled pillars rose under a sky drooping with clouds of huge stone stilettos.

From Superintendent Donald A. Dayton we learned something of the forces that operate to form limestone caves. "The thing to remember," he said, "is that slightly acid water over long periods can dissolve limestone."

At Carlsbad a sea of 200 million years ago built up the vast Capitan Reef complex; subsurface water in succeeding eons carved out the huge rooms. The land lifted, the water table fell below the rooms, and the cave gradually emptied. Then seepage carried in mineral-laden waters that, drop by drop, built the incredible wonderland of thrones and temples and frozen waterfalls in translucencies of stone.

Thoughts of translucence remind me of the "icebox" under Sunset Crater— and beneath the fire-black surfaces of many volcanic fields. Before we left Sunset, David and Steve clambered down into a tube-like cave and beamed flashlights on a blue face of perennial ice. Winter freezes subsurface water, and the overlying lava, a good insulator, keeps out summer heat. Near American Falls, Idaho, along a volcanic rift in the earth that stretches 40 miles, there's an ice cave of great size and beauty. Crystal, it's called, and it duplicates many of Carlsbad's stalactite and stalagmite forms in the splendor of ice.

Many people find enough splendor in trophies brought home from a day's trek on the desert—a piece of shining black obsidian, a chunk of brownish rhyolite spotted with iridescent opal. These rock hounds become rhapsodic over what mere hikers stub their toes on—the region's diversity of stone. The hobby's excitement held us one hot July day when we found a few "thunder eggs," or agate nodules, and geodes at the south edge of the Great Salt Lake Desert. These lumpy, rounded forms—the thunder eggs solid, the geodes hollow—probably formed in cavities created by gas bubbles trapped in molten lava. Very hot water seeping into the pockets deposited minerals: in some, agate layers from top to bottom; in others, agate walls lined with quartz crystals, sometimes in the form of lustrous lavender amethyst. Later the encasing lava weathered away.

Rock hounds also come home with petrified wood, samples of beryl and garnet, and fossils of trilobites from long-vanished seas. Though rock collecting is prohibited in all national parks, it's allowed in some state parks. New Mexico even has one area—Rock Hound State Park near Deming—set aside especially for that purpose. Collectors from throughout the world come with tents and campers and fan out across 250 volcano-churned acres that yield jasper, quartz, agate, and chalcedony.

The splendor of precious metals prompts many men to learn enough geology to go looking for gold or silver or copper. I was in Utah in the wake of the uranium rush that resulted in claims totaling, some say, three times the ore-bearing area. It reminded me of the frustration expressed by a gold miner of an earlier time. He got to Nevada's big Goldfield strike of 1902 after everything was staked solid, so he posted a claim note that read: "I lay claim from this point one thousand feet up in the air. Now beat that you damn land sharks."

The desert's mineral richness derives from a past that knew its ages of fire and of water. A wet time spawned the dinosaurs and laid down the logjams of trees in river bends that in some cases were replaced cell by cell with uranium minerals —the fuel of man's Atomic Age. The realization of such vast cycles of change makes us wonder how many climatic turnarounds the desert country has known.

The answer to that awaits much more research. Evidence abounds that deserts existed 350 million years ago. That's time enough for a grain of sand to count many transitions from rock to dune or water-borne grit and back to rock again.

Largest excavation in North America, the Bingham Canyon Mine cuts a 2½-mile-wide amphitheater half a mile down into the Oquirrh Mountain Range southwest of Salt Lake City, Utah. Here the Kennecott Copper Corporation produces more than 17 percent of the Nation's copper, along with gold, silver, and other minerals. Above, trains creeping along 125 miles of track on the terraces carry waste material and low-grade ore totaling hundreds of thousands of tons a day. Annually, the mine yields 300,000 tons of copper.

Frontiers Past And Present

NDIANS called it the talking wires but were baffled by its humming voice. Pioneers hailed it as the first transcontinental telegraph and jammed it with instantaneous messages that had once taken months. Yet they really didn't understand its song either, for it prophesied an age of technology and the passing of the frontier.

But desert country still contains islands of lingering frontier. We found such an island in western Utah, along the edge of the Great Salt Lake Desert, around a little farming and ranching oasis called Callao. The 40 or so people there have no post office since it was closed eight years ago, must drive 90 miles to a doctor and 40 miles to a telephone, and are just now getting electricity.

David Bagley was busy being host to the annual West Desert Fair, but he took time to let us know that his ranch stood on historic ground. "The first transcontinental telegraph went through here," he said, "and the Overland Stage, the pony express, and the Lincoln Highway."

When the fair ended, the exhibitors departed with their handicrafts, canned peaches, pickles, and prize calves, lambs, and pigs. We joined Mr. and Mrs. Bagley and their four handsome daughters on the screened porch of the ranch cookhouse to share leftover hot dogs, hamburgers, and ice cream sandwiches. Parts of the cookhouse looked very old, and I learned how old when David led me into a low-ceilinged room off the kitchen. "This room was part of the original stage station," he said. "And Mark Twain slept here on his way to Carson City with his brother, who had been appointed Secretary of the Nevada Territory."

Mark Twain was just young Sam Clemens from Hannibal, Missouri, when he rode the stage through here in 1862, but he would put his adventures into a book called *Roughing It* and go on to literary fame. He described the same stretch of desert that we viewed from the Bagley Ranch. The first 45 miles he crossed in the relative comfort of night, Twain wrote, "... but now we were to cross a desert in *daylight*. This was fine—novel—romantic—dramatically adventurous—*this*, indeed, was worth living for, worth traveling for! We would write home all about it.

"This enthusiasm, this stern thirst for adventure, wilted under the sultry August sun and did not last above one hour.... The poetry was all in the anticipation—there is none in the reality....

"The sun beats down with dead, blistering, relentless malignity ... there is not the faintest breath of air stirring; there is not a merciful shred of cloud in all the

Hard-rock miner Martin Duffy, with hard hat and carbide lamp, reflects on his 50-year quest for gold deep beneath the desert of Nevada. The Florence, a mine he bought in 1960, had yielded $9,000,000 early in the 1900's. He died in 1971, still hoping to find a rich seam.

SCLEROCACTUS WHIPPLEI VAR. ROSEUS (UPPER); NATIONAL GEOGRAPHIC PHOTOGRAPHER WINFIELD PARKS

Grubstake loaded on his burro, a prospector pauses for a photograph before setting out from Tombstone, Arizona Territory, in the late 1800's.

Bearded pathfinder John C. Frémont sits for a portrait with his guide, famed Indian fighter and scout Kit Carson, in 1849. In midcentury Frémont led five Army expeditions that provided Congress with knowledge of the mountains and deserts beyond the Rockies.

brilliant firmament . . . there is not a sound—not a sigh—not a whisper—not a buzz, or a whir of wings, or distant pipe of bird. . . ."

We dealt with the reality of that same country when we retraced some of the ten-mile pony express runs. Within the roofless rock walls of relay stations, we stood among ghosts—denim-clad youths racing the whirlwinds, leaping onto fresh mounts with hardly a pause, hastening the mail across the vastness. That experiment to tie together a continent with muscle and sweat lasted only about 18 months, until the telegraph clicked into service in October 1861.

David Bagley gave us a treasured memento of that nostalgic day—a segment of the transcontinental telegraph, a wire that hummed with the keyed pulses of momentous events . . . Lee's surrender, Lincoln's death, the Alaska Purchase.

"We know this place is a bit of history," David told us, "and we're trying to keep it the way it is."

After evening chores David told us why their place had been such an important way-stop: "Water. It was a long, dry ride east and west of here, and there are hundreds of springs and a mountain stream on this place.

"It was an exciting spot at times. After one Indian raid—at Burnt Station, 11 miles away—a soldier rode in here and hollered 'Indians!' then fell off his horse dead. He's buried somewhere up in the field south of the house. My Dad could remember when a little stubbed post marked the grave, but it's gone now."

The Army played a vital role in the taming of the West. Soldiers protected wagon trains and settlers from hostile Indians. Army posts became frontier islands of civilization, with workshops, schools, and hospitals.

As the Army made areas relatively safe, more settlers arrived. Something over a thousand forts were established in the West in the 19th century, some of them little more than temporary tent cities, but others attracted to their flanks sizable communities that survive to the present.

At Fort Huachuca, an old frontier post in the southeast corner of Arizona, now headquarters of the Army's Strategic Communications Command, the past lingers in the old adobe, wood, and stone barracks built in the days when mounted patrols pursued Apaches sweeping down their plunder trails.

The soldiers and officers who manned the forts led lives that alternated between periods of numbing boredom and hair-raising adventure: grooming horses, drilling on hot and dusty parade grounds, standing inspection—and fighting Indians.

"Payday usually came once a month, and the trooper spent all his cash, $9, in one day," said Lt. Col. Bruno J. Rolak, director of the Fort Huachuca museum.

When payday did come the men would head for Tombstone and trouble. A dusty boomtown of shacks, saloons, and gambling houses, Tombstone truly earned its reputation as "the town too tough to die." A stroll down its streets, preserved and restored by its citizens, took us back to the days of blazing guns and boisterous good times before the final close of the frontier.

The railroads thundering across the desert brought that day ever closer. In 1869 the golden-spike ceremony at Promontory, Utah, celebrated the virtual completion of a transcontinental link. By 1883 the Southwest had a line between New Orleans and Los Angeles, and within another ten years the expanding web had gathered in all the principal cities of the area and linked them with the rest of the country.

With the railroads came thousands of settlers who would populate the great inland cities of the desert country. As lines reached into isolated areas, cattlemen could ship out larger and larger herds. Other trunk lines served once-remote mining towns. A traveler could cross the West from Omaha to Sacramento in five days, a journey which had taken stagecoach passengers three weeks.

The 20th century brought the Lincoln Highway through Callao, and venturesome motorists ate dust and sweated over boiling radiators and ruptured tires in a contest to conquer that first coast-to-coast route. David Bagley's father, Cyrene, who was born in 1892 and spent more than 50 years on the family ranch—remembers those early days. "The highway was nothing more than a trail down the old Overland Stage Route," he said. "During high water it was like a trench, with a stream running down it. Over near Fish Springs a man named John Thomas hauled water to maintain his own private mud hole. He'd charge tourists a dollar a foot to pull them out with his team. One man complained that John had pulled him farther than necessary, so John turned his team around and pulled him right back in."

Ranch life was not easy. "We had running water," Mr. Bagley joked. "My wife would say to one of the boys, 'Run get me a bucket of water,' and he would."

Curious about the pioneer's attitude toward the desert, I went to see Sid Brinckerhoff, director of the Arizona Historical Society in Tucson.

"The deserts looked so formidable to the first Americans that they went the other way—to Oregon," he told me. "Why Oregon? Because it was like home. The rains came down on rolling hills with green grass and forests—like Massachusetts or Maryland. The Spaniard had come to the desert and found it to be like home. The American found it to be like hell and often called it that."

To eyes accustomed to a landscape of vibrant green, the wagon trail through Nevada's Humboldt River country required grim superlatives: "The Humboldt was filled with what the Lord had left over when he made the world, and what the devil wouldn't take to fix up hell."

The pioneers cursed the "stinking Humboldt," for as the river twisted across the alkali desert of northern Nevada the waters became increasingly rancid. Still, the river provided a corridor through the rugged hills and bleak mountains.

When the river trickled away into the Humboldt Sink, the pioneers had to brave 40 miles of desert—a blazing furnace in summer—before reaching water.

"The immigrants to California stopped to store water in barrels, and waited till nightfall to start out," explained Victor O. Goodwin, a historian who has covered Humboldt country by jeep, horse, and on foot. "But the hot morning would find them just halfway across the desert, and they would stop because it was too hot to go on. It's terrifying to be out there in that heat. The people would throw away cherished possessions to lighten the load, and back in the 1920's the folks in Fallon, at the edge of the Carson Sink, would make periodic forays into the desert to find old sewing machines, pieces of furniture, children's toys."

The deserts lay across the frontier's path, but the frontier would not stop. To trappers like Jedediah Smith, who in 1826 pioneered a route to the Pacific, the Mojave and Great Basin were just obstacles to getting to the rivers where the beavers were. The following year, leading two companions, a mule, and a horse across the Great Salt Lake Desert, Smith kept a journal of their hardships, telling of "hunger and fatigue and . . . thirst increased by the blazing sands." And he wrote of sleep that "was not repose, for tormented nature made us dream of things we had not. . . . of murmuring brooks, of Cooling Cascades."

To pathfinders like Capt. John C. Frémont, whose interests had swung from exploring to politics, the deserts were an inconvenience in reaching California, where the stage was being set for the 1846 outbreak of war with Mexico.

To Kit Carson, trapper, Indian fighter, and pathfinder, the desert was merely part of the country's challenge. Scouting for Frémont, he did not hesitate to plunge into the Great Salt Lake Desert to find a way across it. Such acts were typical of Carson. A small man, five and a half feet and 140 pounds, he stood ten feet tall in grit and courage. In front of the Federal Court House in Santa Fe, a granite obelisk honors his memory with a succinct biography, in part: "He led the way."

But the thousands who followed the paths west included many who could not measure up to those trailblazers in stamina and boldness. As we drove in comfort over the wide ribbons of paved roads that supplant those trails today, we had for reading matter Irene D. Paden's *The Wake of the Prairie Schooner*, with its many accounts of pioneer desperation.

Her book records the words of Henry Bloom in 1850 as he looked out at desolate flats and thought of loved ones left behind: "I pray God they may never know what it is to want for food, though I starve myself, and there is tolerably good prospect of it right now. What would I not give for some bread, butter and milk!"

"I have noticed several dead horses, mules and oxen by the roadside that had their hams cut out to eat by the starving wretches along the road," wrote pioneer E. S. Ingalls. "For my own part I will eat the lizards which infest the sage bushes, before I will eat the stock that died from the alkali."

With the risks so high, why did those pioneers exchange a settled, provident country for the uncertainties of the arid West? *(Continued on page 96)*

Legendary Judge *Roy Bean, seated on a barrel, holds court at his saloon, "The Jersey Lilly," in Langtry, Texas, near the turn of the century. For 20 years Bean dispensed his own brand of justice at Langtry, a town founded by men who pushed the tracks of the Southern Pacific across the desert.*

Butch Cassidy *and desperadoes of his notorious Wild Bunch pose sedately for a photographer in 1901, shortly after robbing a train of more than $40,000. From left: the Sundance Kid, William Carver, the Tall Texan, Kid Curry, and Cassidy. Pinkerton detectives blanketed the West with this photograph, but Butch and the Sundance Kid kept one step ahead of the law and escaped to South America, where they died violently.*

Ghostly monument *to coal: Madrid,*
New Mexico. Mining families paid a

monthly rent of $2 a room for these
company houses, abandoned when the

Great Depression and natural gas ruined the market for Madrid coal.

SAM ABELL (BELOW)

Century-old *charcoal ovens, each 30 feet high and 27 feet across, stand south of Ely, Nevada. They burned juniper and piñon to produce charcoal for a silver smelter at nearby Ward.*

Screening dirt *for buttons, shotgun shells, coins, and other small objects, University of Nevada anthropologist Dr. Richard H. Brooks excavates a miner's campsite of the 1890's. The artifacts he and his students discover receive detailed study at the school.*

Climber rappels *down the* Tinajas Altas, *or High Tanks, just above the Mexican border in southwest Arizona. In an area where much of a year's rainfall can occur in one sudden afternoon cloudburst, these tanklike formations become natural reservoirs, holding rainwater for several months. Such water holes saved many a forty-niner along the nearby* Camino del Diablo—*Devil's Highway*—*when it was the main route from Mexico to California. The desert trail claimed the lives of some 400 people.*

"I call it the land of best chance—or last chance," Sid Brinckerhoff had told me. "Some saw an opportunity here that couldn't be resisted, a chance to get rich in mining or by provisioning the cavalry. Low-cost land drew many. Others were running away from something, a failure in Ohio or a tragedy in Illinois. For all who came it really was the last frontier, and the most hostile."

The West was rich in precious metals, and successive bonanzas fetched hordes of humanity this way and that, into some of the most forbidding land on earth, spawning overnight cities of planks and tents and dugouts. "The miners wanted the good things of life that people had back East," said Brinckerhoff. "Many of our ghost towns are marked by thousands of empty champagne bottles and oyster cans."

We became seekers of boom-time relics among the crumbled foundations and abandoned mine entrances of once bustling Gold Hill in western Utah. Its mines had produced first gold, then copper and some silver and tungsten. Today the creaking of rusty hinges and the whispering of the wind are the only sounds.

We had a metal detector to help us, but we found the place already well gleaned. All we came up with were a few worn-out horseshoes, a faded Prince Albert tobacco can, and a fierce thirst that started in the tongue and reached to the toes. We cured that by retreating to the base of the mountains, where Tom's Creek—as cold as snowmelt—came splashing out of a canyon. Chill as the water was, it took a few seconds for my superheated body to feel it, and my head felt feverish until I ducked beneath the current. Surely we absorbed moisture through our very skin!

Folk in off the desert, whether miners, stage drivers, or trappers, hit town with prodigious accumulated thirsts and hungers and layerings of dust. Their impatience to be served probably explains a sign in early Tucson: "Don't shoot us. We're doing the best we can." Barbershops made extra money by providing bathtubs and hot water in the back room. And one enterprising barber advertised, "Ears washed without extra charge."

If adjusting to the land was hard, adjusting to the Indians in possession of it proved even harder. For me, the chronicle of misunderstandings, disputes, massacres, and wars is best expressed in the bitter story of the Apaches—especially the band known as the Chiricahuas under their great chief Cochise.

Take any road north or east from Tucson today and you're in Apache country. We angled east past the Dragoon Mountains to the Chiricahua Range. Switchbacks and blind curves led up to a promontory that hung over the desert like a balcony, then the climb gentled into a ponderosa-shaded fastness called Rustler Park.

To such secret retreats the Apaches would vanish from desert skirmishes below, to rest and cauterize their wounds and live to fight again. It was a guerrilla tactic proven in centuries of opposing superior numbers of Mexicans and Pueblo Indians. "The Indians could travel a hundred miles a day, and keep it up for a week over the difficult terrain of rugged mountains and bleak desert," said Dan L. Thrapp, a *Los Angeles Times* editor who has crisscrossed the region studying and recording Apache history since 1958. "The Army found it almost impossible to track down a raiding party. The Apaches knew every water hole and could carry water stored in cow intestines and wrapped around the necks of their horses."

In their early dealings with the Americans, the Apaches sought to make friends with the White Eyes. They distinguished between the newcomers from the East and the Mexicans, who so long had been an enemy. War leaders even offered to join Brig. Gen. Stephen Watts Kearney and his Army of the West in the Mexican War.

Cochise, too, hoped at first for peace with the Americans. Contemporary accounts paint him as a tall, stately, finely built Indian who seemed to be rather past middle life, but still full of power and vigor, both physical and mental. Then his people were wrongly blamed for the kidnaping of a child. Cochise parleyed with an Army representative at Apache Pass under a flag of truce. When the Army leader threatened to hold Cochise hostage, he drew his knife, slashed the tent, and fled. Cochise escaped, and for the next years the Apaches made Arizona and New Mexico "about the liveliest places on God's footstool."

According to Cavalry Capt. John Bourke, the cost to the United States was "ten thousand men, women, and children killed, wounded, or tortured to death, scared out of their senses or driven out of the country, their wagon and pack trains run off and destroyed, ranches ruined, and all industrial development stopped." Nearly every family lost a member or friend to the Apaches in the 1880's, Sid Brincker hoff told me. "It was a period of uninterrupted, incessant, daily warfare, when families lived in terror day by day of ambush and murder."

In 1886, with the capture of Geronimo and his band of Chiricahuas, the Army won its war with the Apaches, and life on the frontier became a less venturesome business. It had been a struggle of many separate explosions, with the Indians often choosing to die rather than yield. Captain Bourke described one such fight to the death when soldiers surprised a small band and bottled them up in a cave. Bourke's Indian guides and interpreters raised the cry: "'Lookout! There goes the death song; they are going to charge. It was a weird chant. . . half wail half exultation. . . .'"

"'Lookout! Here they come!' Over the rampart. . . . Our men rushed to the attack like furies. . . . Six or seven of the enemy were killed . . . and the rest driven back within the cave. . . ." The soldiers resumed a furious fire, aiming at the cave roof to bounce bullets down onto the defenders. Finally a detachment on a cliff above began to drop boulders that avalanched into the cave.

When the troops charged the cave they found 76 Indians dead or dying. "These were probably Yavapais and not Apaches," said Mr. Thrapp, "but to many frontiersmen all bad Indians were Apaches."

At last the wars ended, and the Apaches came onto the reservations. Treatment varied with the Army officers in charge, and with the successions of Indian agents and contractors—good and bad. Bourke recorded one chief's complaint: "When Major Randall was here we were all happy; when he promised a thing he did it. . . . others have come to us since he left, but they talk to us in one way and act in another."

Cochise had died in 1874, during one of those interludes of brittle peace, and his followers buried him in secret, to frustrate any who might make a show of his bones or regalia. At first the secret intrigued me, and I pressed area historians for clues to his resting place. But my questioning was futile, and to my surprise I began to prize my failure. It seemed good that this old fighter should find in death the tranquil refuge that eluded him in life.

While most settlers went west looking for the best land, one group went looking for unwanted land. The Church of Jesus Christ of Latter-day Saints—the Mormons—had encountered enmity and violence in Ohio, Missouri, and Illinois. Only the huge and mysterious West seemed far enough away from civilization to offer sanctuary. California and Oregon still held vast bountiful tracts, but Mormon leader Brigham Young rejected such attractive prospects, preferring instead to look for a place no one else would have.

With David Bigler of Salt Lake City, who's deeply interested in his Mormon heritage, I threaded the same Wasatch Range canyons that posed the final barrier to Mormon wagon trains winding from the Missouri to the Great Basin. Approaching from the northeast, we at last stood in the saddle of Big Mountain and gazed through a maze of peaks into the Salt Lake Valley, the migrating Mormons' tentative goal. Here the advance party paused in 1847 and gave way to exhilaration.

"We waved our hats and shouted Hossanah," Orson Pratt wrote in his diary. When Young and the main party wound down Emigration Canyon, he stopped and, according to tradition, announced, "This is the place."

People with less faith might have had doubts. Once the Mormons set foot out of the mountains, they walked in desert. Young himself spoke of barren valleys, sterile mountains, and desolate waste. But, as David Bigler explained it to me, "When the Lord gives you His word, through the prophets, there is only one thing for you to do: literally, to build an earthly kingdom of God."

This willingness of church families to accept colonizing missions was the real secret of Mormon success in the desert.

At first the kingdom-building didn't look too hard. Seven streams rushed out of the Wasatch Range, sources for irrigation. And the land—though scruffy with sagebrush and bunchgrass—proved rich in potash and other minerals.

By the spring of 1848 some 1,700 people were building homes and planting crops. Wheat, corn, and beans thrived, and pasture grass grew thick. Then, on Sunday, June 4, John Steele wrote in his diary: "There has come a frost which took . . . nearly everything, and to help make the disaster complete the crickets came by the thousands of tons, and the cry is now raised, 'we can not live here, away to California.'" But veterans of the Mormon Battalion, just arrived from service in the Mexican War, Steele wrote, almost to a unit declared, "'God had sent us here, and here we were going to stay, come weal come woe.'" Then gulls came and devoured the crickets, and the people thanked God for a miracle. Today that gratitude lives on in a monument in Salt Lake City's Temple Square, world center of the church. Atop a narrow lofty column two golden gulls alight on a golden orb.

During the first lean winter, the settlers grubbed for anything edible, picking seed pods from roses and thistles, and digging up the bulbous roots of sego lilies. But the kingdom's methods began to work. Common effort was the key. It sprang out of their faith in a common goal—the building of the New Zion. Water and timber rights could not pass into private ownership, and irrigation must develop logically and jointly to serve whole watersheds. These would be among key points urged decades later by explorer John Wesley Powell, who implored the Nation to pass special homesteading laws to fit the special requirements of arid regions, but to no avail. Thousands of settlers moved west.

Then came the reckoning: recurrent drought. It began in the 1870's and lasted until the turn of the century. The whole Southwest baked and shriveled. The overstocked range withered, the cattle industry collapsed, and thousands of animals perished. Sheep, first introduced to the West by the Spaniards, died during the drought too, even though they were better suited to desert living than cattle. Fond of shrubs and easily moved to higher grazing areas as spring advanced, they usually flourished in arid areas.

The pioneers who endured such times became self-reliant. They had to. "There was no frosting on the cake," Chris Fox told me in El Paso. He was born when the Army still stationed most of its cavalry in New Mexico and Arizona, and he grew up to become El Paso County sheriff. Through the years he has become a student of the frontier days.

"If your neighbor was in trouble," Chris said, "you went to help him. You knew that if you didn't, no one else was liable to, because no one else was around."

It was a lonely life for men, lonelier for the women. But resourcefulness, community spirit, and hospitality were human qualities that rode westward with the frontier—and they tarry wherever the frontier spirit lingers. That's why I find so much to like in desert people.

Muscles bulge with strain during the 1971 weight-pulling contest at the National Basque Festival, held the first week in July every year at Elko, Nevada. While his friend Manuel Izaguirre counts cadence, winner Juan Vicandi drags a 1,400-pound concrete block 63$\frac{1}{2}$ feet in five minutes. Many of the estimated 60,000 Basques in the American West today descend from men who came from the Pyrenees in the mid-1800's to tend sheep on the open range. Some of the older Basques remain in the sheep business, but most modern immigrants, like Juan Vicandi, take jobs with construction companies or in factories.

The Kingdom of God on earth, Mormons called this valley when they emerged from Emigration Canyon on July 24, 1847, to look down on the site of present-day Salt Lake City. The monument, sculpted by Brigham Young's grandson for the 1947 Mormon centennial, marks the place where Young first saw the valley and, according to tradition, said: "This is the place." Escaping religious persecution in the Midwest, the Mormons traveled a thousand miles west from Winter Quarters, now Florence, Nebraska. They stopped at the edge of the Great Salt Lake, irrigated the fertile valley, and turned the desert into their promised land. From 1847 until the completion of the coast-to-coast railroad in 1869, nearly 80,000 of the faithful migrated west along the Mormon Trail in wagon trains like the ones opposite. Here in Echo Canyon, Utah, the pioneers pass the transcontinental telegraph, finished six years earlier in 1861.

Towering figure of the American West, Brigham Young supervised the migration of thousands of Mormons to the Great Salt Lake area. Elected president of the Church of Jesus Christ of Latter-day Saints in 1847, he later served as the first Governor of Utah Territory, from 1850 to 1857.

Beauty and Harshness In the Desert World

LONELY EMPTINESS, seemingly infinite distances, boulders shimmering in the heat— these belong to the desert world. Musing upon this awesome realm, naturalist Joseph Wood Krutch wrote: "To some it seems merely stricken, and even those of us who love it recognize that its beauty is no easy one. It suggests patience and struggle and endurance. It is courageous and happy, not easy or luxurious. In the brightest colors of its sandstone canyons, even in the brightest colors of its brief spring flowers, there is something austere."

Light rules here with indescribable brightness. The clear air conspires with light, so that distant horizons are magnified; peaks a hundred miles away appear near at hand. Nor does the conspiracy cease at sunset. Desert mountains and thunderheads reach for the retreating light, and give it back to earth as gilded afterglow. Later, stars reign with astonishing brilliance. "I saw a faint shadow one night when there wasn't a moon," a Utah man said, "and finally decided it was being cast by Venus. At first I couldn't believe it."

People seek the desert for solitude, for renewal of health and spirit. Tiring of overcrowded cities, they may come for a holiday and remain a lifetime. There are wind-rippled dunes to wander, and multihued canyons to explore. Desert hikers can camp in the shelter of cottonwoods, or climb to a mesa's ridge and watch the morning sky change from gold to deepest blue. Old-timers and newcomers alike must continuously be amazed at the abundance of wildlife they find, from minute puddle-dwellers to pupfish, from kangaroo rats to mountain lions.

The desert's parched, forbidding aspect has in the past been its best protection against encroachment. Today, however, thousands of people are drawn to the desert lands. Resort and retirement communities spring up beneath perpetually clear and sunny skies; motorcycles and air-conditioned campers track the salt flats and sands. And increasingly Americans come to realize the value—and vulnerability —of their remaining desert wilderness.

Like a mirage become reality, an 18-mile-long lake covers salt flats in Death Valley, driest spot in the United States. A lake of such size, occurring perhaps once in a century, results from heavy rains. This one, formed in February 1969, disappeared by late August.

*S*hifting dunes of gypsum, sculpted by the wind, cover White Sands National Monument, New Mexico.

Rows of tumbleweeds, plants that scatter their seed by rolling before the wind, has become a major nuisance on some farm and range lands, spread from Canada to

flank a man and his horse on a road in Sonora. The Russian thistle, a tumbleweed that

Mexico within 25 years after its introduction with flax seed imported from Europe in 1874.

Seabirds race their shadows across the Pacific off the coastal desert of Baja California. Aloft from their nests on barren rocks, they cruise the shallow, rippled waters for small fishes and shrimp — morsels many capture with spectacular dives.

*M*ilitary aircraft pattern the desert at Davis-Monthan Air Force Base near Tucson, kept from damaging corrosion by the hot, dry air. Some yield spare parts; others await return to active use. The same Arizona climate that protects the planes also attracts people. Sun City (left), a growing retirement community of some 23,000 near Phoenix, requires at least one family member to have reached the age of 50, and allows no resident children who have not finished high school.

Heading for Las Vegas, more than 150 miles away, motorcyclists begin the San Gabriel Valley Hare and Hound Race at Barstow, California. Within a few miles 3,300 riders will begin funneling into a rugged trail six feet wide. "It's a challenge," declared one entrant. "The desert terrain is always a little rougher than you are." Conservationists, however, deplore the scarring of the deserts by such recreational activities.

Plants: A Tenacity For Survival

VELVETY, MOIST PETALS trembling in the desert breeze. Succulent green leaves and stems shadowing time-varnished rocks. Explosions of color against the dry country's grays and tans and whites. A seeming paradox of nature: bright blossoms amid shrubs brittle with desiccating heat; touches of paradise in a parched, sun-tortured purgatory.

No matter how often we came upon fields of desert flowers, the sight always affected us deeply. It seems somehow miraculous that in so hard a land phacelias bloom as purple as Indiana irises, yellow poppies carpet a forbidding hill as if it were coastal Oregon, pale, fringed ghostflowers carry the gingery fragrance of Carolina carnations.

To many, such vivid blossoming seems an impossibility. The desert, viewed casually, appears hostile to any kind of life. But those who know it are thoroughly aware that life exists there—and exists abundantly. Dr. Frits Went, director of the University of Nevada's Laboratory of Desert Biology in Reno, is such a person.

"Plants and animals survive in the desert in one of two ways," he told us. "Either they endure their arid environment, or they escape it." The annuals escape through their seeds, which sleep the droughts away, for perhaps a decade, maybe even longer. They awaken only to the right cadence of rain and temperature, conditions that promise time for them to sprout, flower, and produce seed before the moisture runs out and doomsday heat begins.

"The insects that pollinate the blossoms somehow appear when the blooming occurs," Dr. Went said. "They must respond to the same triggering devices, and more than moisture must be involved. The whole complex subject needs investigation."

While science ponders the possibilities, our family won't be idle. We'll scout the plains and hills at every opportunity for more floral gardens. And if we ever hear of the whole desert awash with blooms, as rarely happens, we'll turn our lives upside down to see it, for that is an experience that has eluded us.

We've come close: sweet-scented sand verbena in Utah's sandstone mesas, Indian paintbrush scarleting a high sweep of Nevada mountain valley, spikes of prince's plume clinging to Colorado canyon slopes. And there was a sun-drenched October morning when we left Panther Junction in Big Bend National Park, Texas. We wanted to spend the day in Boquillas Canyon, where the Rio Grande begins to knife through a massive wall called Sierra del Carmen. But we got only about three

Golden halos *from the setting sun fringe saguaros towering above teddy bear chollas on a hillside in Tucson Mountain Park, Arizona, part of the Sonoran Desert. Like all plants of the desert, the saguaro cactus has adapted to extremely high temperatures and minimal water.*

miles before we braked to a stop beside a field of lemon-yellow blossoms—ground-hugging limoncillos. Their delicate flowers loaded the breeze with a lemon-like scent.

Garnishing the visual feast were tiny rose-magenta star flowers called windmills, and some shin-high daisylike bladderpods, all set amid low desert brush turned vivid green by recent rains. Gray and purple mountains filled the skyline. It was a time for being pleased with things just as they were, and we lingered and made it last. The Rio Grande had to wait.

There was a similar day in Utah canyon country when our jeep wound among pockets of white evening primrose on red sand, and a morning in Baja California when blossoming globe mallow turned a seaside plain to orange and light green.

My particular heroes in the drama of desert survival are those plants that must endure year after year. The perennials have adapted in a multitude of ways to withstand the harsh challenges of the desert. Their persistence is a tremendous testimony to one of the most vital forces in our world—the fierce tenacity of life.

Of all the desert perennials, I reserve my greatest admiration for the many members of the cactus family. Native to the Americas, they have diversified into more than a thousand species and have developed functionally into shapes so distinctive that the mind can never forget them. Some bear tasty edible fruit, and shelter or otherwise help sustain many creatures of the desert community, including man. They bloom with an extravagance of color, and during their time of flowering the desert wears them like gems.

"You can say we got very close to the cactus family," Virginia told me as she debarbed herself for the umpteenth time. Getting stuck was an experience we all shared, at one time or another, without any lessening of affection for these rooted porcupines. The jumping cholla posed the sharpest test for Virginia; she's convinced that one really jumped at her. "It did! I didn't come closer than a foot from it, and it got me," she insisted.

Indeed the cactus, along with a similar species, the teddy bear cholla, does seem to leap at its victims. Devilishly barbed spines arm jointed stems on the shrublike plant, which thrives over wide areas of the Sonoran Desert. The breakaway joints hook a ride on any creature that makes the slightest contact—hence the belief that they jump. If you ever do become impaled, at least you'll have the dubious satisfaction of knowing you're helping to propagate these chollas, for under the right conditions of soil and moisture the joints will take root where they fall.

The cactus wren nests among the cholla's continuous armor of spines and hops nimbly about without getting stuck. We awoke one morning in southern Arizona to find a nest builder busy in a chin-high plant by our campsite, and we watched anxiously, fearing each second that she would stab herself as she wove a pouchlike nest deep in the cholla's branches. Nearby a male worked as busily, building another nest. He might roost in it, and the female, too, but she would lay her eggs only in her own feather-lined home. The male's model may be a decoy, for the maze of cholla spines does not entirely deter predators in search of eggs—ground squirrels, snakes, and curve-billed thrashers.

Besides admiring all the varied members of the cactus family and getting stuck by more than a few of them, we used them for shade, burned their dried skeletons for fuel, ate a sugary cactus-pulp candy, and employed a cactus segment to hasten the settling of sediment in muddy drinking water. The last experiment came as a suggestion from Beaver Bill Howland of Green River, Utah, who earned his nickname by trapping on the Green and Colorado Rivers early in this century. "Slice open the pad of a prickly pear cactus," he advised, "then use it like a paddle to stir your bucket of water. When we run sheep up the Green to mountain country, we move and break camp every day. We need to settle the river water quickly, and this works best." I tried it with interesting results: The silt seemed to coagulate into tiny lumps and settled rather rapidly. In a couple of minutes the water was translucent, if not clear, a definite improvement over the old just let-it-stand method.

Say the word "cactus," and many people get a mental picture of a thick, straight-up trunk with rounded tip, and sturdy branches curving to the vertical in a candelabra effect. The species responsible for this image is a local monarch of the family, the patriarchal saguaro of southern Arizona. In some 200 years of slow growth, it may attain a height of 50 feet and a wealth of holes and scars from the creatures it helps to shelter or feed.

This mammoth cactus begins life so precariously that it needs "nurse plants" to ward off killing sun and frost in its first tender years. Dr. Rod Hastings of the University of Arizona told me of one nurse tree, a paloverde, that shaded two saguaros through their early stages, then paid for its services with its life. It happened in Sonora, Mexico: "My colleague Ray Turner and I saw this dead paloverde suspended between two young saguaros. They apparently grew up into its branches and pulled its roots right out of the ground."

But the saguaro nurtures far more than it kills. White-throated wood rats—pack rats—nest at its base and, on rare occasions, eat its pulp. They have been known to tunnel upward to lofty balconies near the top, thus hastening the death of the host plant. The Gila woodpecker and gilded flicker make numerous nesting holes, and the saguaro heals the wounds by growing a callus more lasting than the cactus itself, surviving on the desert floor long after the giant has fallen. "The desert is the only place I know where you can go for a walk and come home with a hole for a souvenir," commented naturalist Joseph Wood Krutch.

After the hole-makers move out, a succession of occupants move in—elf owls, flycatchers, purple martins, sparrow hawks. They all take advantage of the saguaro's excellent insulation; when the temperature in the sun tops 110° F., nest holes register a reading about 20 degrees cooler. In a land of few trees, red-tailed hawks build their nests in the forks of lofty branches.

On warm May nights the ghostly white of the saguaro's flowers is matched by a flutter of alabaster wings as white-winged moths arrive for a meal of nectar and some pollinating chores. The long-nosed bat and many insects also come to dine. When the juicy, egg-sized fruit ripens in midsummer, Papago Indians carry on the tradition of the harvest, using long poles to reach the branch tips.

On the Papago reservation just southwest of Tucson, we went to the gleaming white mission compound of San Xavier del Bac to ask Father Kieran McCarty about the Indians and the saguaro. He serves the tribe as padre and historian, reflecting his Franciscan flair for scholarship; his stub of cigar and turtleneck sweater reflect his flair for informality.

"The saguaro harvest was the time of plenty, the first month of the Papago calendar," he said. "It was a time when the people would camp among the saguaros until they had gathered all the fruit. Then they would hold a big celebration."

Early in this century explorer Carl Lumholtz wrote of the saguaro's importance to the Papago: "Not only does the fruit . . . furnish them with their principal means of subsistence, but the greater part is boiled down to a sirup for future consumption

Creeping devil, or *caterpillar cactus,* moves across the Magdalena Plain in southern Baja California; the photographer's guide avoids bristling spines by using a stick to examine one of the plants. Continuously taking root at one end, the cactus actually inches forward, the rear shriveling and dying as the front grows. When the plant encounters a rock, fallen log, or another cactus it creeps up and over it.

Blossoming yellow in spring, a blue paloverde flourishes in the Sonoran Desert. The rock wall of Cerro Cubabi looms behind the tree and a neighboring saguaro (left) and an organ pipe cactus. Dependent on a good underground water supply, the blue paloverde grows in washes and canyons throughout the desert lands of Mexico, California, Arizona, and Colorado. It reaches a height of 30 feet and in summer produces beans once used as a food staple by Indians.

in the winter, serving also as material for an intoxicating drink, which is used at the sahuaro festival. The seeds . . . are eaten after having first been ground on the metate, and they taste better than would be expected. . . . The wooden skeletons or ribs of the sahuaro furnish . . . light, strong, and elastic building stuff. . . . Even the wooden tissue bags produced by the woodpeckers are made to serve as water bottles or drinking vessels."

In a land of little and uncertain rain, how could a saguaro live long enough and get big enough to do all this? For one thing, it is the camel of the plant world. One of these giants may absorb as much as a ton of water during the short season of rains and conserve it for the dry seasons and for droughts.

I learned that a thirsty saguaro is like a starving man—the ribs show. Vertical columns of wood beneath the ribs support the massive plant. In dry times the grooves between the ribs deepen, fluting the stem. When the rain is more plentiful the cactus absorbs water and expands, the surface becomes taut, and the flutings are less prominent.

Under the unrelenting desert sun, leaves become a luxury because they are water spendthrifts. The cactus family has largely given them up. A green hue reveals the presence of chlorophyll in the stem, which for the cactus takes over the process of photosynthesis—a role leaves perform for most other vegetation.

To draw upon solar energy, the versatile cactus must, of course, use the days; but in absorbing carbon dioxide, it has another trick for beating the heat. To get the vital gas, it must open its surface pores, and as the carbon dioxide enters, moisture escapes. So to minimize water loss, the cactus takes on carbon dioxide at night, when temperatures are lower and the humidity higher.

All members of the cactus family are succulents, moisture-heavy plants able to store water for long periods. The hoarding of moisture seems such an efficient means of desert survival that you might suppose most desert plants would be succulents. The fact is, most are not. The lily family includes a non-succulent that rivals the cactus in evoking the desert's spell—the yucca.

Early in our travels, Dr. Stanley L. Welsh of Brigham Young University made us aware of the yucca's vital role for many southwestern Indians: "It was perhaps their most important noncultivated plant. They ate the buds, the young flowers, and the stalks. They plaited leaf strips into baskets, mats, and sandals. They made very fine sandals, as well as rope, out of the twisted fibers of the leaves."

The basic yucca silhouette is a rosette of long dagger-shaped leaves topped by a mastlike stalk and bearing a large cluster of creamy flowers. Yuccas grow from southern Utah and the Great Plains to deep in Mexico, from west Texas to the Pacific, and they vary both in form and size. Pioneers called them Spanish bayonets, for their leaf shape, or soapweed, because the roots and stems yielded a soapy substance for laundering. Though most range from 6 to 15 feet tall, a species known as giant dagger in Big Bend Park has a flower stalk that may reach 20 feet. An even larger form has become the trademark of the Mojave—the Joshua tree.

Joshua Tree National Monument, about 150 miles east of Los Angeles in the Mojave Desert, protects these strangely beautiful plants, which rise above sandy slopes, rocky outcrops, and endless miles of shrubs. Twisted arms reach 15 to 40 feet into the sky from a thick trunk and branches thatched with dead, grayish leaves. A burst of short, stiff green leaves crowns the tips of the branches. Each year some leaves wither and die to become part of the shaggy matting below as a new ring of foliage emerges at the top. According to one local tradition, Mormons gave this giant yucca its common name because the arms recalled Joshua beseeching Heaven for victory. *(Continued on page 128)*

Amber ants *crawl across a lava flow speckled with yellow lichens (Acarospora schleicheri) in the Valley of Fires State Park, New Mexico. These lichens, among the more common ones in the desert, thrive on shadowed rocks.*

Panamint daisies *two feet high blossom in May in a side canyon of Death Valley National Monument. One of the desert's rarest plants, this flower grows only in the Death Valley area.*

Hummingbird *seeking nectar hovers near an agave in bloom in Big Bend National Park, Texas. The agave, or century plant, does not produce a flower stalk until after some 15 years of growth. Some species bloom only once, then die within months. Found throughout the southwestern deserts, agaves provided food, drink, soap, medicine, and rope fiber for Indians; today, the plant still yields fiber, as well as tequila, pulque, and industrial alcohol.*

Scampering *toward its nest in the Sonoran Desert in Arizona, a white-throated wood rat — or pack rat — grasps a cholla joint in its mouth. Hundreds of bits of cactus help make the rodent's quarters a spiny fortress that protects it from many predators.*

Diversity *of plant life rises from a carpet of late-summer grasses in the Sonoran Desert in Organ Pipe Cactus National Monument, Arizona. Despite an annual rainfall of only a few inches, 537 known species of plants exist in this 516-square-mile preserve.*

Cactus wren *perches on a jumping cholla in Arizona near the entrance to its dwelling of dried grasses; the bird's nesting area extends far into the plant. The cactus may have taken its name from the fact that cholla spines stick to passersby at the slightest contact.*

Sipping nectar *from a flowering saguaro, a white-winged dove ducks its head into a large blossom. At night, when the cactus first opens its petals, a long-nosed bat hangs near a flower before lapping up nectar with its tongue. Such creatures fertilize the saguaro cactus by spreading pollen from plant to plant. Towering as high as 50 feet, saguaros may survive as long as two centuries; water may comprise as much as 95 percent of their bulk. In gathering all available rainfall, the cactus extends a wide-spreading root system just below the surface. Even in the driest of years, saguaros blossom and bear some fruit. But of perhaps 12 million seeds produced by a saguaro during its life, according to arid-land specialist J. R. Hastings, only one may survive to develop into a mature plant.*

Papago Indian *reaches high with her harvesting stick to gather ripe fruit from a saguaro near Tucson. The Indians eat the sweet, pulpy fruit raw, boil it into a syrup, or use it to make a fermented drink.*

Most species of yucca are wholly dependent for their survival upon a small creamy moth, and the moth, in turn, is dependent on the yuccas. "The pollinating moth lays its eggs in the flower," botanist Stanley Welsh explains, "and the yucca reciprocates by providing seeds for the moth's larvae."

A trip to New Mexico in late June makes clear why the yucca is that state's official flower. What began for us there as a lazy desert holiday became a pilgrimage from bloom to bloom as each new flower-crested stalk seemed fuller, taller, and more exquisitely set against sky and mountain. We agonized a long time over which photograph to reproduce for our Christmas cards. There's a Spanish name for the yuccas that helps explain our feeling: *cirios del Señor*, candles of the Lord.

For the uninitiated, the yucca has a twin—the agave, and both have met the problem of survival in a similar way. Our exuberance over a flash of iridescence and a blur of wings led us to our most memorable encounter with agaves. We never caught up with the hummingbird, but he led us to an area studded with agave blooms in Baja California's dry Desierto de Vizcaíno. The first plant we came to had a 12-foot mast that flew no fewer than 32 yellow flower clusters, each bigger than my hand. Bees gathered the nectar in a frenzy of energy. For us, the beauty and flurry had a touch of poignancy, because we knew this might be the agave's only fling. After growing and manufacturing resources for 15 years or so, some species of the plant stake it all on one extravaganza of blooming and seeding, then die within a few months. Other species send up new sprouts from the roots or from the axils of the lower leaves. The agave is also called the century plant from the legend that it takes a hundred years to get ready for a single flowering. Once the bloom stalk starts, it may grow as much as 16 inches in 24 hours.

There is a rarely-seen desert flower that opens almost fast enough for the eye to perceive it. The night-blooming cereus stores a hidden water supply in its tuberous root; the stalk is so spare that Spaniards called it "dead stick." Most of these plants bloom on a single night in summer. Like many nocturnal flowers the cereus combines luminous whiteness and strong fragrance to announce itself to pollinating moths and other insects.

Plants that cannot hoard water compensate in a variety of ways, existing nearer the edge of survival and exploding into spurts of growth and seeding when rains come. The creosote bush, for example, though it depends on erratic rainfall for its periods of growth, has spread over vast desert acres, from the edges of the high sage country to the torrid coastal plains.

Even at night you can tell when creosote bushes are near, because you can smell them—and that explains how they got the name. The Mexicans call the bush *hediondilla*, little stinker. Though some may find the scent somewhat unpleasant, I happen to like it. To me it's somewhere between the resinous smell of a pine forest and a freshly tarred roof.

I particularly remember a showery April day when we pulled to a roadside in Arizona to watch a cloud show; a swirling gauze of mist was playing meteorological sleight of hand with the Papagos' sacred mountain, Baboquivari. As we stepped out on the damp desert sand, Virginia asked, "What's that smell? Has the road been freshly oiled?"

It hadn't. We were downwind from a slope of creosote bushes, deep green and glistening wet, and loading the moist air with their rich incense.

The smell derives from a resinous coating on stem and leaves. Water gathered through a wide-spreading shallow root system can't be squandered away into bone-dry air. The covering adds a varnished sheen to young twigs and tiny green leaves. In a good flowering year the bushes put out numerous yellow blooms, each no larger than a quarter. But the eye gets a total effect of ethereal hue, yellow mist afloat above a pavement of tawny rocks or volcanic cinders.

For desert survival, the creosote bush uses one trick that has stirred debate for many years. Mature bushes appear to eliminate competitors so effectively that their spacing is often parklike, as if they had been planted. Some studies suggest that they kill rival creosote plants by secreting a poison into the soil. The poison doesn't appear to affect any other vegetation. But how could it kill creosote seedlings while sparing older plants?

Dr. Lillian Sheps, of the Laboratory of Desert Biology, is hard at work on the question. The young botanist divides her time between the laboratory on the University of Nevada campus at Reno and field trips for more data.

"Many plants produce these growth-inhibiting substances," she told me, "and the creosote bush is an interesting example. It seems that the quantity of inhibitor secreted by the mature plants is enough to kill seedlings but not enough to kill older plants." Seedlings that germinate close together, but away from older plants, usually survive, she has observed. Those that germinate naturally under mother plants almost always die in less than a month. She has confirmed this pattern by transplanting seedlings under mature bushes. All of them soon died. Others, transplanted in open ground, had a better survival rate.

Some authorities, although they concede that certain plants secrete substances that may inhibit growth, believe that competition for moisture is the major factor in the even spacing of creosote bushes.

Dr. Sheps readily agrees that the problem is a complex one. "I'm also studying the role of desert fungi," she said. "Adding a mulch of dead leaves and branches containing the fungi seems to help the plants survive. Is there a relationship between the chemical substance and the fungi? Perhaps. It's one of the many aspects we have to investigate. There are many factors other than water, important as it is, at work in the desert, and we simply don't know enough about what they are."

But one thing is certain: It takes very little extra moisture to make a remarkable difference in the growth of desert plants. We saw a dramatic demonstration of that fact while driving across a great gray slope of creosote bushes in the northern end of Death Valley.

"Look, it's as if a hedge lined the road," Virginia said. The plants at roadside, nourished by water runoff from the blacktop pavement, stood distinctly taller than those across the desert, and as neatly as if they had been shaped by a gardener.

Actually, it takes but one paved road to show how easily man can alter nature's balance. Over much of west-central Utah one August week, we found highway shoulders rippling with the egg-yolk yellow blooms of wild sunflower and the rosy-pink fluff of beeplant. Fed by the drainage off the road, this narrow strip was a micro-environment ribboning the desert, a visual treat amid the gray-green shrubs of the Great Basin.

Sagebrush spreads in profusion through wide valleys and up gentle slopes in patches of soft, lustrous color. In the cool of evening, a sagebrush fire brings contentment and warmth to any camper. The wood burns pungent and clean, snapping and crackling with an energy that sends sparks dancing into the dark pool of night. Several species of sagebrush and many look-alike members of the saltbush family dominate the floor of the high-country deserts; but their growth was not so widespread before the pioneers arrived. These shrubs have invaded overgrazed ranges, covering land shorn of its natural grasses.

Even trained scientists can alter the ecological pattern, despite their precautions. Dr. Kimball Harper of the University of Utah told me of the deep chagrin he once experienced with a colleague, Dr. Edgar Kleiner of the University of Nevada. They were investigating a crusty dark material that crumbles into dust under the pressure of a foot; actually the crust is a complexity of life forms—up to a dozen kinds of algae, fungi, lichens, and other minute plants. It retards erosion by wind and water and increases the fertility of the soil by drawing nitrogen from the air.

"Edgar and I were being very careful," Dr. Harper said. "We even walked in each other's footprints to minimize the damage to the crust. When we returned a few months later, we got a shock. In each of our footprints there were seedlings—mostly annual buckwheats. We had compressed the soil, and when rain came, water ponded in our footprints, producing an environment favorable to the germination of the seeds."

Almost any mountain canyon high above the desert may support woodlands of oak, juniper, and piñon pine along its sunny walls, and Douglas fir and western yellow pine in the more shaded areas.

Constant seeps of water sometimes moisten alcoves in the canyons, spawning a luxuriant profusion of plants, including orchids, monkey flowers, and columbines. With the water problem solved, the fight is for a place to root and a place to stand in the sun. Every crack becomes a foothold for the persistent roots, and vegetation often forms heavy draperies of green down the stone walls, in an effect called a hanging garden.

I went to see a hanging garden one day in Utah's Arches National Park. It came up to expectations, except that I was a bit early in May for much blooming; only a few columbines raised their sceptered light-blue heads.

But a deep emerald pool at the foot of the cliff was a disappointment, a small fraction of its former size. The roots of huge cottonwoods and a heavy growth of willows had once stabilized a natural earth dike, but the trees had been cut by beavers. Now the dead roots lay exposed by erosion, rotting and breaking away. I had always listed dam-building beavers on the side of the conservationists, but here I saw them as despoilers, however innocently.

Naturalist Joseph Wood Krutch decided that as a botanist he fitted a category labeled "much given to exclamations of wonder." Exclaiming over strange plants is not an objective, scientific thing to do. There was a time when botany tempted me as a profession, but I'm glad I didn't yield to it. If I had, I'd be bound now to a more clinical, disciplined approach to the plant world. As it is, I'm free to go where I will and wonder as I will about the many marvelous things that plants do to survive.

The boojum tree is a case in point. From the time I encountered the name I felt sure it would be a worthwhile thing to see. My goal was fixed when I learned that it grew only in two very limited areas—around Puerto Libertad in Mexico's Sonora state, and in Baja California. I would go to Baja California.

A boojum by any other name—and it has another name, *cirio,* or candle—would look as weird. Picture a giant parsnip with a stubble of twiglike branches, a lightish-gray root standing on its head and sticking its tapering body 20, 30, even 60 feet above ground. Some boojums put out two or three branches near the top that sometimes grow upright and sometimes don't. Occasionally, both tree and branches curve down, intertwining crazily with themselves or nearby trees into incredible pretzels against the sky.

The name boojum came spontaneously to the man who bestowed it. The year was 1922, and engineer Godfrey Sykes of the Carnegie Institution's Desert Laboratory was exploring the coastal Sonoran Desert near Puerto Libertad. One afternoon he trained his telescope on a distant hill and for the first time beheld the

Night-blooming cereus spreads delicate petals and stamens on a summer evening near Tucson. Most of these nocturnal plants flower only during a single night in June; their fragrance attracts bats, birds, and insects. A large tap root —measuring up to 20 inches thick and weighing more than 40 pounds—acts as a reservoir for water. Sparsely distributed through the Sonoran and Chihuahuan Deserts, the night-blooming cereus grows in the shelter of larger plants.

BILL AND MARY LOU STACKHOUSE (ABOVE AND BELOW)

Radiant hues of cactus flowers splash North America's deserts with color. A trio of golden blooms, each three inches wide, sprouts from a prickly pear, a cactus with paddle-shaped branches. Blossoms of the barrel cactus (upper left) nestle among curved spines at the top of the plant. Yellow stamens contrast with the red petals of a prickly pear (far left) that grows in small, low clumps. Like scarlet sunbursts, petal-like flower parts of the red-flowered hedgehog open at the ends of funnel-shaped floral tubes. A yellow bloom spreads its petals beside an unopened bud on the branch of a cane cholla, a cactus that grows four feet tall.

strange tree. For a few moments he gazed wordlessly; then, as naturalist Krutch recorded, his son Glenton heard him exclaim:

"Ho, ho, a boojum, definitely a boojum." For an out-of-this-world sight, he had reached into the other world of Lewis Carroll, whose *The Hunting of the Snark* mentions an imaginary creature or thing called a Boojum, an inhabitant of far, lonely, desolate coasts. ". . . hence the name given on the spur of the moment by Godfrey Sykes was perhaps appropriate," his son concluded. It was not merely appropriate, it was unforgettable.

The first ones we ever saw that were of the classic shape drew us right off the road. We were some 300 miles into the peninsula when we caught sight of the unmistakable profiles against a steep hill. Many visual curiosities suffer from over-promotion, so that the actual first sighting is a disappointment. But not the boojum. "Doubtless God could have made a queerer tree . . . but if He did I have never heard of it," Krutch wrote.

I had always wanted to meet this eloquent spokesman for the boojum, but his zestful life came to an end about a year before I began my travels westward. Nonetheless, his writings provided our text for the day. When we wondered how to convey the worth of a tree that does not feed you, hardly shades you, and makes lumbermen sneer, we turned to Krutch on the boojum and read: "But it does have individuality and character and they both mean something in terms of its success in a country where only extraordinary organisms can survive. What looks like grotesque perversity is actually a logical adaptation to needs, and a functionalist can hardly deny it one kind of beauty."

Point by point, the boojum scores high on the desert-survival checklist: vast shallow root system, semi-succulent trunk, thick light-colored reflective bark, small leaves, little wind resistance in a land of savage winds. It apparently grows very slowly, displaying that almost incredible ability to endure that stamps most living things in this harsh land.

Despite their occasional gymnastic branchings, a desert filled with nothing but boojums might be a trifle monotonous. But the traveler seldom finds them alone. They grow interspersed with a variety of vegetation—huge cardon cacti, looking much like the saguaros and surpassing them in mass, small blond-spined chollas, and another of Baja California's botanical specialities, the *torote*. Its low-growing trunk flings out many thick, bulging branches, and in the dry season their gnarled limbs claw the windy sky. The torote, better known as the elephant tree, has grayish bark and clubby limbs suggestive of elephant trunks.

I think back to a cool February night when we camped in the lee of huge granite boulders and watched a full moon escape the many black fingers of an elephant tree, leapfrog a cardon, and graze a boojum before gaining the open sky. Its timing was just right to entertain us while we cooked, ate, and sipped coffee close to our fire's dwindling warmth.

Though the boojum's family tree is still being investigated, plant genealogists say it's in the same family as the ocotillo of the Sonoran Desert. The more familiar ocotillo raises a score or so of thin, supple, spiny stems, some nearly 30 feet high. They spread outward and in spring fly extravagant orange-crimson flowers that bob in the breeze like perching tropical birds. Mexican farmers and Indians use the pliant stems for arching shelter supports and for fencing. I will not forget passing a primitive rancho in Sonora and seeing a palisade of ocotillo that had taken root and provided a living corral that was crested with bloom. It was the most beautiful fence I have ever seen.

Our youngest son John doesn't always share our admiration for desert plants, because he finds that most of them flunk his basic test: "Is it good for climbing?" There are two types of desert trees that under good conditions attain size enough to be climbed, paloverdes and mesquites.

In April the Sonoran Desert wears its paloverdes like golden fleece. Yellow petals cling to the generous branches and dazzle the eye with brightness in the warm sun. But I became a fan of the paloverde because of its beautiful bark. The tree's Spanish name translates "green stick," and that pale green hue means photosynthesis is going on during the dry season, independent of any leaves. The tree does in fact put out small leaves in times of rain, but it sheds them during dry spells and depends on the stems for survival.

This genus includes one member with blue-green bark, the blue paloverde, which produces a remarkable seed that sprouts only when conditions for germinating are close to ideal. The reason is a special cover that is abraded away by sand and stones when the runoff from summer downpours catches the seed and hurtles it downstream. It is freed to germinate only after repeated scouring by rushing water. The root tip first aims downward, to provide a good base. Only then does the seedling rise to challenge the hostile air.

Many a mesquite never becomes more than a scrub, but those that get their roots down to a dependable water supply achieve great girth and age. We spent a day and a night in a patriarchal grove below Death Valley's Grapevine Mountains beside a trickle of cool water called Mesquite Spring. These members of the pea family grow formidable spines, but the spines have long since dropped off the principal limbs of large trees. They branch low, inviting young climbers aboard, screening out the sun and letting the breeze whisper through.

Like the yucca and saguaro, the mesquite provides much for the life around it. For the Shoshoni Indians and other tribes in the lowland desert, its branches provided shelter and fuel. The Indians relished the raw bean pods and also ate the seeds fresh, cooked, or dried and ground into meal. One kind, the western honey mesquite, bears pods from which they could extract a sweet, nutritious syrup. From the fibers of the roots and bark the Indians made beautiful baskets. Its gum served as glue, dye on pottery, and as medication for such ills as sore throat.

Some people say the mesquite doesn't really qualify as a true desert plant—because in the most arid regions it grows only along washes and in other drainage areas, or where its roots can reach deep enough to tap subsurface moisture pockets. One miner reported running into mesquite roots 175 feet down.

I know this: The desert traveler will do well to find a supply of dead mesquite wood for his campfire. It ignites readily, burns hot with little smoke, and the embers last. Like hickory, it imparts a special taste to food. When we came to mesquite thickets in Baja California, we gathered dead wood to make sure that our evening camp would not lack for its cheery flames. For Christmas one year Jesse Gilmer, a friend in El Paso, Texas, sent us a side of bacon cured with mesquite smoke. When we dropped a few slices in the skillet the aroma brought back desert sunsets and dinners simmering over glowing coals. And the bacon had flavor to match.

On a nature trail in Saguaro National Monument near Tucson, I overheard a youngster's remark that stuck in my mind: "If I lived in the desert, I'd want to be a cactus." I believe I know just what he meant; he had sensed that the cactus is equal to the challenges hurled at it by a hostile environment. He had cut through the tendency of most newcomers to look at the hard land and feel pity for any life that must exist there. I would carry the boy's thought a step further. For here is the truth that every old desert hand knows: *All* the plants and creatures that live there have adapted well to the difficulties of survival and are very much at home.

Bristling with thorny twigs, cirios, or boojum trees (left), command the heights above the Gulf of California in Sonora. The tapering trunk, containing soft, spongy pulp that can retain large amounts of water, thrusts as high as 60 feet. Boojums, named after the weird creatures or things imagined by Lewis Carroll for his book The Hunting of the Snark, grow only in Baja California and in a limited area of the Mexican mainland.

Malformation resulting from disorganized tissue growth (above) deforms a cactus in Organ Pipe Cactus National Monument. The abnormal development —called fasciation, or "cresting"— causes enlarging and flattening of the branches of many species of cactus.

Greenish-white blossoms tip the rough branches of Joshua trees in Joshua Tree National Monument, California. The preserve, one of many throughout the southwestern deserts, provides protection for hundreds of species of plants and animals. Found in the Mojave Desert area, Joshua trees sometimes grow 40 feet high.

Animals: Adaptation In a Harsh Land

BEFORE LUNCH one hot June day, I wandered away from our camp in Utah, lured by the beauty of an orange- and cream-colored canyon. I left my canteen behind since I planned to scout around for just a short time. But one crook in the trail led to another and I ended up exploring beyond every next bend. The sun climbed higher, and I soon became so parched that my craving for water controlled all my thoughts.

It was then—after three hours in the sun—that I fully appreciated a fact I had learned earlier about a furry little desert dweller: Throughout its entire lifetime, the kangaroo rat never needs to take a drink of water. In arid regions that greatly simplifies life.

Most desert animals—from ants to bighorn sheep—are masters at simplifying life. They are equal to the extremes of their environment and survive through special adaptations, like the kangaroo rat's.

Many other rodents, reptiles, and even some birds share the distinction of never needing a drink of water—providing they get their proper diets—but the kangaroo rat is celebrated for it.

Although called a rat, it is closer kin to the pocket gopher, with a plumpish profile that makes it look well fed even when starving. As the kangaroo rat gathers food, it accentuates the rotund effect by packing its external cheek pouches with rations. Big black eyes, helpful for night vision, are prominent in an overly large head. Diminutive forelimbs, adapted to stuffing seeds into its pouches, give the creature a hesitant gait. But when it needs to make a quick getaway, it rears back on powerful hind legs and bounds off.

"Did I just see what I thought I saw?" asked an astounded Virginia one dark evening. I'd swung off the road to turn around after making a wrong turn, when three—or was it four?—little dervishes on springs hopped into and out of the track of our headlights. Each rodent was on its own heading, bouncing like a Ping-Pong ball and seeming to change course with each landing. The display ended so fast that we had to reassure each other it had happened.

The leaps spanned some 30 inches and crested at about a foot and a half, a typical performance for any of a score of kangaroo rat species. Most of the animals are less than a foot long, and most of their length is in the brush-tipped tail. It serves as a rudder during jumps and assists in the erratic course changes.

Kangaroo rat nibbles grain in the glow of red lights; zoologist Joseph De Santis at the Southwestern Research Station near Portal, Arizona, part of the American Museum of Natural History, studies this rodent, a nocturnal creature that can go a lifetime without a drink of water.
OCOTILLO (FOUQUIERIA SPLENDENS) UPPER

Mottled coloration camouflages a Texas horned lizard resting in midday sun in New Mexico. Shielded from predators by spiny scales and a horny crest, the lizard can also squirt blood from the corner of its eye when highly excited. The six-inch-long reptile, commonly called a horned toad, eats a wide variety of insects and especially favors ants.

Wary eye peers from among beadlike scales of a 20-inch Gila monster — only poisonous lizard in the United States.

Pointed scales on the hind foot of a fringe-toed lizard help it to scurry across loose sand by providing more traction. When pursued, the eight-inch-long reptile burrows into the sand to hide.

At the Philip L. Boyd—Deep Canyon Desert Research Center west of Palm Desert, California, I talked with David Grubbs about the desert adaptations of the nine-inch-long Merriam's kangaroo rat—the species spotlighted by science. Popular attention has centered on its ability to manufacture water from a diet that consists overwhelmingly of air-dried seeds.

"But this is an oversimplification that fails to emphasize the real adaptations to the desert environment," said David, a doctoral candidate at the University of California at Irvine. He's conducting a field study on the energy and water relationships in the bodies of desert rodents, including the kangaroo rat. "When any animal burns a unit of carbohydrate, fat, or protein, it obtains a fixed amount of water. So if someone says an animal can live on its metabolic water, they're really saying its mechanisms for water conservation are so good that the animal can live on the water it produces and not require any to drink."

And the kangaroo rat is not just conservative but downright miserly when it comes to expending water. A remarkable kidney is part of the answer; it produces urine three and a half times as concentrated as man's. If the human kidney worked as well, we could drink sea water and safely concentrate the extra salts for elimination. Also, its nasal anatomy permits the kangaroo rat to condense and recapture the moisture from its own breath as it exhales.

The kangaroo rat's miserliness spills into all aspects of its existence. Except for bounding away from danger, it avoids energy sprees. It's nocturnal; if you see it in daytime, chances are you've caught it in an emergency—forced from its deep burrow by a predator. Most of the time it stays in a comfortable microclimate underground, coming outside for perhaps an hour or two at night. It may spend several weeks underground, eating stored food. The kangaroo rat's humid burrow provides protection from daily and seasonal temperature extremes. In summer its deep home is a cool retreat, in winter a place of warmth.

"It avoids the stresses that would cost it significant amounts of water," David summarized. "Like many desert creatures, the kangaroo rat is an escapist."

All small desert mammals must be escapists, avoiding daytime heat since they cannot afford to use up the water needed for evaporative cooling to prevent critical rises in body temperatures. In *Desert Animals,* a classic study of heat and water problems, Knut Schmidt-Nielsen reports that several kangaroo rats were exposed to an air temperature just under 110° F. "Their body temperatures increased rapidly," he recorded, "and they all died within 45 minutes to an hour and a half."

A healthy man, however, could hike in the desert at the same temperature with no ill effects, providing he could replace his sweat loss—about a quart an hour. But water replacement he must have, or he too will die.

Investigating the myriad survival stories of desert creatures, we found a wide variety of solutions to the heat and water problems. But in the kangaroo rat and man we found opposite approaches: the rodent a careful conservationist that cannot dissipate heat rapidly, and man an admirable heat-releasing machine as long as he has plenty of water.

The chisel-toothed kangaroo rat—a species that lives in the Great Basin—differs markedly from other kangaroo rats. Like man, it cannot survive without an external source of water. Dr. G. J. Kenagy studied this rodent while working on his doctorate at the University of California at Los Angeles.

"The chisel-toothed kangaroo rat forages in the tops of saltbush shrubs, stuffing the leaves of the plant into its fur-lined cheek pouches," he said. "Returning to its burrow, it grasps the leaves individually and draws them over its broad lower incisors, scraping off the very salty exterior tissues and discarding them. Left behind

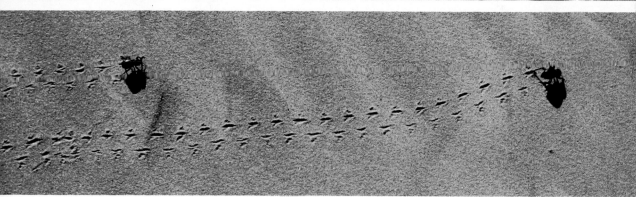

Tarantula *—its bite painful but its venom not deadly to humans—covers the back of a man's hand in Big Bend National Park. Female tarantulas can live as long as 25 years and have a seven-inch legspan; the smaller males often fall prey to females after mating.*

Pinacate beetles *track sand flats in the Gran Desierto of northern Sonora; their thick shells seal pores and joints, minimizing evaporation. When threatened, the inch-long wingless beetles stand on their heads and wave their hind legs in a bluff display to ward off enemies.*

is the juicy, much less salty interior portion of the leaf that supplies the rat with water, starch, and protein—all the nourishment it needs."

Our boys' favorite desert citizen is not a rodent but a bird—and a star of animated cartoons at that. The roadrunner, although it can fly, does so reluctantly, preferring to sprint on long legs. Judging by the frequency with which it races across the desert, matched against a fleeing lizard or a bouncing jeep, the roadrunner likes to run. Our son David, encountering his first roadrunner in Daylight Pass above Death Valley a few years ago, felt positively honored to have taken part in a foot race—and lost!

Two feet long and mostly tail and legs, the roadrunner is no beauty. Markings around the eyes look like carelessly applied mascara, and the bird has a feathery topknot which it raises abruptly when alarmed. We decided that this member of the cuckoo family contributed greatly to the clan's reputation for zaniness.

But despite its comic demeanor, the roadrunner is a creature admirably adapted to survival in the desert. Nimble legs enable it to catch a host of insects and lizards while eluding birds of prey such as the red-tailed hawk. The bird can outmaneuver, outwit, and outlast a rattlesnake in battle, sometimes to the death, a proficiency that earns it a distinctive nickname, "snakebird."

The roadrunner has an ability to take advantage of the desert's most abundant form of energy—sunlight. "When air temperatures are low, this bird substitutes the heat of solar radiation for heat generated by body chemistry," Dr. Robert D. Ohmart of Arizona State University reports.

"The roadrunner nestlings have solid-black skin, quite different from other desert birds," Dr. Ohmart says. "The color permits them to absorb good quantities of solar energy. They hatch in late spring or early summer when nights and early mornings are cool and lizards—the staple food of the young birds—are abundant. The nestlings use the heat of the sun in the early morning hours, replacing the warmth provided through the night by the parents, which have left the nest to hunt whiptail lizards for their young.

"The platform nests are usually located in a cholla, and when the sun gets too warm, the nestlings align themselves with shadows cast by the thin branches. They also dissipate body heat through gular fluttering—vibrating the throat area with the mouth open. During gular fluttering, as in sweating, heat is lost through evaporation of body fluids; but salts are concentrated in the remaining fluid. Roadrunners void these excess salts through a nasal gland; many marine birds have this adaptation, but the roadrunner is one of the few land birds that share it.

"As adults, roadrunners retain the black skin color on their backs. Whenever air temperatures are cool, the birds obtain energy by putting their backs toward the sun and raising the feathers that cover the black areas. When they have soaked up enough solar radiation to warm themselves, they lower their feathers."

No matter how well a creature has adjusted to aridity, the coming of rain to the desert enhances the prospects for continued life and helps create a chain reaction of activity. "When good summer rains fall, large numbers of insects appear, sparking increased feeding activity throughout the desert community," Vincent Roth told me. He directs the American Museum of Natural History's Southwestern Research Station near Portal, Arizona, a scientific facility tucked into an awesomely vast canyon of the Chiricahua Mountains. "Termites pop out of the ground and the adults are ready to fly; right along with them come red mites, a quarter-inch-long or more. They feed on the termites.

"Then toads, which have remained dormant near the surface, emerge and start feeding on the insects. The hognose snake appears and feeds on the toads, while kit foxes and ring-tailed cats have a change from their diet of lizards and rodents.

"And the large predators—coyotes, bobcats, mountain lions—complete this extensive food chain by devouring many of the other animals."

When rain falls at the right time to make the desert bloom—usually in mid-July—bees, wasps, moths, and butterflies mysteriously come forth to carry out pollination chores. Lloyd Tevis, research associate at the Deep Canyon research center, theorizes that the insects emerge at the time the plants flower largely because of water penetration into the soil. The rain, which under just the right conditions triggers the growth of the annuals, soaks down to the dormant insect life, signaling a brief era of plenty. Beckoned by favorable circumstances, such creatures prosper briefly, propagate the next generation, and either die or return to dormancy, waiting on the thin edge of existence until the desert flowers again.

Such, too, is the life of the toad. In the desert, toads lead an existence very different from that of their cousins in more humid areas.

"Like all amphibians, the toad doesn't take water through its mouth as we do, but literally soaks it through the skin," Dr. Rodolfo Ruibal of the University of California at Riverside explains. "In the desert, the toad continues to use this same mechanism, but must search much harder for water. Since it cannot depend on a convenient puddle of water or a pond, the toad must burrow down to damp soil, where it can maintain water balance just as it would in a Southern swamp."

To span periods of drought, toads go underground and remain for months in a torpid state, their systems rationing out life energy. After talking with Dr. Ruibal, I could better appreciate the wild choruses of toad voices that fill the darkness on those rare nights when pools of fresh rainwater pocket the desert. For me, the music is exultation, the same joy that sounds in the cry of northbound geese as they fly high against the moon on a spring evening.

"The salamander is strictly an opportunist," Dr. Walter G. Whitford of New Mexico State University told me, speaking of another desert amphibian. "Unlike salamanders I studied back East, the ones that live in New Mexico apparently can breed whenever they have water, thus helping to assure the continuance of the species. These amphibians also retain gills so long as there is enough of a pool to swim in. As the water dries up they lose their gills, switch to lung respiration, and become land dwellers."

While the salamander can live in or out of water, a rare desert cockroach draws water directly from the air. Dr. Eric Edney of U.C.L.A. has extensively tested the nymph and adult stages of *Arenivaga investigata* and discovered that it absorbs significant amounts of moisture from unsaturated air. "Such a phenomenon has been observed in ticks and mites," Dr. Edney said. "It's unusual in insects, but clearly useful for those which, like this one, live among sand dunes."

Paradoxically, much desert life depends on the existence of an aquatic environment. Death Valley's Salt Creek and Cottonball Marsh harbor tiny colonies of inch-long pupfish. The species apparently survives from the Ice Age, when a 90-mile-long freshwater lake filled the continent's deepest trough. But now, pupfish thrive in water that varies from near fresh to three times the salinity of the ocean. Other groups of pupfish in the nearby Amargosa Valley, in the Salton Sink, and in the Sonoran Desert cling to life in pools that hardly amount to teardrops compared to the immensity of the sere world that surrounds them.

But the desert cradles even more precarious aquatic life. Potholes in huge slabs of rock catch the rains and become little realms of life, some hardly larger than goldfish bowls, that last only a matter of days. In that brief time, however, a whole system of life appears, from microscopic algae *(Continued on page 152)*

WILLIAM L. ALLEN, N.G.S. STAFF (ABOVE)

Ten-inch-high kit fox perks its big ears and attentively stares as it detects motion—possibly prey—near its home in the Sonoran Desert of Arizona. Acute hearing serves better than smell in dry desert air, which evaporates scents. During the day, these shy mammals usually laze in dens they have built in soft soil, occasionally among the roots of a tree or cactus; at night they hunt lizards, insects, rabbits, and rodents—especially kangaroo rats—by running them down or digging them out of the ground.

Ears cocked, a mule deer doe tests the air for scents while browsing on leaves in Great Sand Dunes National Monument, Colorado. Prevalent in brush and cactus country, the six-foot-long deer can sprint at 35 miles an hour.

Sleek coatimundis hunt food among the branches of a paloverde tree in Arizona. Over the past 50 years, the gregarious creatures have extended their range into the United States from Mexico. They feed on small mammals, insects, and birds, as well as on roots and berries. A furry, two-foot-long tail equals the length of the creature's body.

Bushy-tailed Harris ground squirrels curl up in their underground burrow in the Arizona-Sonora Desert Museum near Tucson after a meal of grain and cactus. The ten-acre exhibit area of the museum houses hundreds of species of desert mammals, reptiles, insects, birds, and plants, most in natural settings.

Coasting on a current of air, a red-tailed hawk scans the Sonoran Desert of Arizona for rodents, snakes, and insects in this representation of desert plant and animal life on an early morning in July; the hawk's mate guards their nest in a towering saguaro cactus. During the morning and late afternoon of such summer days, many desert animals, particularly birds and reptiles—but also a few mammals—hunt for food. By midday, however, most retire to shade or their burrow to wait out the severe heat. This painting groups together more creatures than would ever likely assemble in such a limited area. In the endless struggle for food and moisture, some animals compete for the same source of nourishment. A 20-inch-long chuckwalla lizard poised on a rock seems startled by a Yuma antelope squirrel; both have sighted the hedgehog cactus near the rock. The chuckwalla, one of the largest North American lizards and a vegetarian, can thwart pursuers by darting into a crevice and inflating itself like a balloon, frustrating attempts to dislodge it. Near the squirrel and chuckwalla, a roadrunner dangles a freshly killed lizard. A beetle in its beak, a cactus wren perches near its nest on a branch of chain fruit cholla. Collared peccaries—each weighing as much as 45 pounds—feed near creosote bushes. With their elongated snouts, they root in the soil for tubers and insects. A foot-long desert tortoise stretches its neck to munch on the pad of a prickly pear; the reptile obtains most of its liquid needs from such succulent plants. Gliding over a pile of cholla joints gathered by a pack rat, a western red racer seeks the entrance to the rodent's lair. With a higher heat tolerance than many other snakes, the racer can search for food during the middle of the day. At the rim of an anthill, a regal horned lizard eyes harvester ants. The squat creature can flick out its tongue and swallow an ant before the insect has a chance to bite.

PAINTING BY JAY MATTERNES

Darkness and the cool of a summer evening rouse a variety of nocturnal animals, including most of the large mammals, from their inactivity during the day. Adapted to night feeding, such creatures use keen vision and the cover of darkness to advantage. Wings spread wide, a great horned owl drifts above the desert floor, seeking prey. With a silent dive, it will grasp a small mammal in viselike talons and return to its nest in a saguaro. Below the owl, a 25-pound bobcat tenses as it detects a white-throated wood rat, or pack rat. Wiry strength, stealthy hunting habits, and sharp claws and teeth make the bobcat a formidable predator of small birds and mammals—and an occasional deer. The pack rat, carrying a cholla joint—both food and building material—hurries back to its nest. A spotted skunk, chewing on a giant desert centipede, spots a kangaroo rat crouching by the hedgehog cactus. A tarantula on an insect-hunting foray creeps from under a rock. Sliding over the same rock, a large western diamondback moves in to swallow a rock pocket mouse it struck earlier. The snake tracked the rodent until it finally dropped and died. Another rock pocket mouse gathers seeds, and a pack rat bites into a prickly pear as predators approach from either side. A Gila monster stalks past the prickly pear while a ring-tailed cat lurks near the white blossoms of a night-blooming cereus. This animal's bushy tail grows to 17 inches—equal to its body length. Bounding just yards ahead of a coyote, a black-tailed jackrabbit zigzags through the underbrush, trying to evade its pursuer. The jackrabbit can sprint to speeds of 45 miles an hour and cover more than 20 feet with a single leap. Flying above the coyote, a big brown bat zeroes in on an insect, forming a scoop with its tail membrane to snare the prey against its chest. The bat will then flash its head down and eat the insect.

PAINTING BY JAY MATTERNES

to water striders and fairy shrimp. For his doctoral dissertation at the University of Utah, Steven V. Romney monitored 25 potholes in southeast Utah, checking them at least once every two weeks. His working stance is a low crouch, like a Moslem at prayer, flanked by scientific apparatus for measuring such variables as temperature, acidity, and dissolved oxygen content. But I found him wielding one tool that didn't seem so scientific: a sieve—"this very crude and barbaric instrument I've been living with for two years."

With a single dip of that sieve, he nets tens of thousands of bits of life. "And sometimes you get 60,000 diatoms—algae—in a single liter of water," Steve said. "Once the pothole fills, these life-forms develop in a very orderly way, the smallest first. The algae must be ready for the larvae of the mosquitoes or shrimp to feed on. Otherwise the food chain breaks down."

And as the water in the pothole is sucked into the dry air, the complex community transforms to a state of arrest, usually as eggs, but in a few instances as pupae. As a crusty dark coating on the dry pothole walls, the dormant life must endure months, and maybe even years, of alternate baking and freezing.

Whenever I pass a dry pothole now, I speculate as to how many experiments in life lie locked to its sides. And when I come to a filled one, I look for the water striders, the whirligig beetles, and the tadpole shrimp to tell me that this precarious world of life has gambled one more time—and won.

After dinner one evening in Arizona, my family and I lazed by the campfire watching ants systematically carry away crumbs scattered from our supper. To us, they looked like the same ants that win the race to the potato salad in a backyard picnic at home, but we learned that there are some fascinating differences.

I talked about honey ants with the husband-wife research team of Drs. George C. and Jeanette Wheeler at the Desert Research Institute in Reno, Nevada. "Honey ants gorge certain members of the colony from an early age," Jeanette told me. "Such a member clings to the nest ceiling and is stuffed with liquid food or water until the hind part of its body becomes huge—the size of a pea. When food becomes scarce, the colony calls upon these overstuffed members, termed repletes, to disgorge their stores and feed the other ants. This specialization has been observed only in these desert species."

In the course of my travels I also learned about differences in food-gathering techniques of the desert-dwelling ants in the Joshua Tree National Monument. Whenever food is plentiful the ants forage at random. But, when supplies become scarce, they forage as an organized group, going out in a slightly different direction every day and systematically covering the area. Eventually, they complete a sweep around the nest, like a radar scan in slow motion, making an overall survey of food availability and taking full advantage of it.

Another technique the ants use is recruit foraging. Scouts go out searching for food, and once they find it they return to the colony and recruit workers to gather it. The scouts usually lay a chemical trail that leads the workers back to the discovery. In this way, a colony can mobilize quickly to take advantage of a large source of food, such as a dead animal or a fallen cactus fruit.

Ants, too, are among the large body of escapists, avoiding the sun at its hottest. They simply move to a lower level of their extensive tunnels as the heat increases, thus maintaining a more or less constant temperature-humidity environment—a form of air conditioning that burrowing animals often employ. Many desert lizards also seek shade or a burrow during the heat of day. Even though they are cold-blooded creatures and need the sun to help control their body temperature, they must guard against too much heat, for its effects would be lethal.

The chuckwalla, a big lizard almost 20 inches long, feeds exclusively on vegetation. But a friend of mine once discovered a specimen with a strange passion. "A big one appeared at our camp in Grand Canyon one morning, and we couldn't figure out what he wanted," reported Ron Smith, a partner in Grand Canyons/Canyonlands Expeditions. "So I gave him a cigar. He puffed on it and seemed to like it and after a while was back for another. Well, I could see he was almost addicted on just one cigar, and it would have been wrong to let him have a second. So I made him kick the habit right there."

The skin of the chuckwalla droops from its body in great folds and wrinkles; it has a sagging stomach and even a double chin. But it wears this oversize suit for a reason. Any severe fright sends it scurrying into a rock crevice where it inflates itself like a great balloon by gulping in mouthfuls of air. Wedged tightly among the rocks, the lizard is almost impossible to dislodge; it will even allow part of its tail to be pulled off without deflating itself and trying to escape.

Changes in the chuckwalla's skin color during the day help regulate its body temperature. In the cool of first light, it turns dark to absorb more solar heat, but as the day warms it becomes progressively lighter to reflect the sun's radiation. This color shift might also serve as camouflage.

Other lizards have permanently changed their color to match their surroundings. In New Mexico's White Sands, lizards have evolved into a near-white race to blend with the gypsum dunes, while lava beds a few miles north are the home of dark lizards that merge with the color of the volcanic rock and cinders.

Anyone who has ever tried to run in deep sand will appreciate the adaptations of the fringe-toed lizard and the sidewinder rattlesnake; both of them seem to move effortlessly in loose sand. The lizard's fringes are actually small pointed scales on the back of its toes and along the lower parts of its legs; the scales work much like the treads on a snow tire, covering a greater surface area and giving the creature better traction in the sand.

The locomotion of the sidewinder is more puzzling. The snake forms its rather short body, usually not more than 18 inches, into a flowing "S" and then moves sideways in an easy fluid pattern. Its body leaves a discontinuous track, one part made by the upper half of the "S" and the other by the lower. The head, middle, and tail do not touch the ground. Students of this technique say half the body thrusts forward for new purchase while the other half holds ground, a sort of body-walking system. I find the motion of the sidewinder to be almost mesmerizing, but not to the extent of letting the snake approach too closely—it has a venomous bite.

Actually, the chances of being bitten by a rattler or a Gila monster or of being stung by a scorpion have been exaggerated. Like most rattlers, the sidewinder prefers to run or hide, striking only if cornered or startled. When I commented to Vincent Roth at the Southwestern Research Station that I had seen few snakes during my travels in the desert, he replied, "Yes, but a lot of them have seen you."

Rattlers differ individually and by species and can never be counted on for automatic retreat. Mr. Roth illustrated this fact: "If three people walk single file past a black-tailed rattler, chances are that all three would pass without being bitten. If the snake happened to be a western diamondback rattler, it might bite the third person in line. If it was a Mojave rattler, which I consider the desert's most aggressive snake, it would probably strike at the first person."

The Gila monster, the only venomous lizard in the United States, is slow and timid, and has to chew into its victim to inject poison. In the deserts of Mexico and southern Arizona and New Mexico, scorpions pose a threat, and one species (*Centruroides sculpturatus*) is highly venomous. But a bite or sting from any of these creatures will rarely kill an adult. The venom, however, might kill a child, or a person allergic to it.

Most of the large desert animals are mammals. Generally, they adjust to heat and lack of water like all other creatures—by foraging for food when it's cool and conserving their energy in shade or burrow when it's hot.

The collared peccary—or javelina—follows such a schedule. During the morning and in late afternoon, the 16-inch-high, 45-pound relative of the domestic pig browses and digs into the ground with its elongated snout, rooting up tubers and insects. Feeding in this manner, it turns and aerates the soil, functions vital to the continuance of life in the desert.

Traveling in herds for protection, peccaries must live within the reach of permanent water. Their sharp hooves cut distinct paths as they make their daily trek to water holes or springs, where big predators such as mountain lions and an occasional bobcat often lie in wait.

Though the coyote, a nocturnal hunter and scavenger, may sometimes attack a young peccary, it preys mainly on rodents and rabbits. In early evening, I have often heard this wily member of the dog family break the desert stillness with its eerie howls. During the hotter hours, it holes up in its burrow, or in a convenient shaded spot.

Scrappy hunters, bobcats roam a territory of five or six square miles at night, stalking small mammals and birds. Desert species of bobcats have a paler and thinner coat than their woodland cousins; they also grow to smaller sizes, thus demanding less food and conserving more energy. Compact and wiry, bobcats are fierce fighters and have an unpredictable disposition. Naturalist John James Audubon once cared for a two-week-old kitten and found it "a most spiteful, growling, and snappish little wretch."

One of the most effective diggers in the desert is the squat, striped badger. With its short, powerful legs and sharp claws, it can burrow quickly into crusty soil, easily chasing down a ground squirrel or kangaroo rat tunneling ahead of it. Because of the energy it expends in chasing its prey, the badger devours large numbers of rodents, insects, snakes, and birds. A thick layer of fat guards the badger's internal organs from the sun's heat, and it usually holes up in a cool burrow at midday for further protection.

It's hard to get a good look at what I think is the dry country's most majestic animal. The desert bighorn sheep spots you a mile away and prudently retreats from view. Its eyes register movement keenly, but if you pick a spot in the rocky parapets overlooking a chasm and remain patiently still, you may be rewarded by the sight of a ram on a crag, a three-quarter curl of horn crowning a head profiled against the clouds.

I found good sheep country above the Deep Canyon research center where Jack Turner, a young graduate candidate, patrols the heights to amass data on the animals. He has trapped a few and attached radio transmitters to them; these homing devices enable him to find the herds with a minimum of searching. A large, high-fenced pen at the research center encloses a few study animals.

"This is Gumdrop," Jack said, introducing a ewe that trotted straight to him and nuzzled his hand. "She has one love in life and that's sugar." He fished for a lump in his shirt pocket and fed it to the sheep.

The large animals cannot burrow underground, so they have developed other methods for coping with the heat. Desert bighorns can store heat during the day. "Their normal temperature is 99° F.," Jack told me, "but when the day is hot they can let it rise to 105° without ill effects. When night comes, and air temperature drops below the body temperature, the sheep begin reradiating the excess heat."

In comparison, man must maintain his temperature near the normal of 98.6° F. During the scorching day, this requires the loss of water through sweat; at night, he begins to burn energy to keep warm as soon as air temperature falls below his normal temperature.

The sheep have protective devices that guard against absorbing too much heat, however. Like man, they disperse heat by sweating—as much as their heavy coats allow. By taking quick shallow breaths, the sheep draw air over a heavily veined area in the throat, cooling blood that is carrying excess body heat.

"During the spring they tend to put on extra fat, especially along their backs," Jack told me. "These layers of fat provide excellent insulation against summer heat. Also, burning off the fat releases extra water into the system."

But nature surely must have committed an error, I thought, in programming the bighorns to mate in August, a month when desert days are long and fiercely hot and the forage is scarce. In ritual battles, the rams square off and charge each other, butting heads in stunning collisions that echo off canyon walls like dynamite explosions. Since these displays cost the animals great amounts of energy, it seemed that nature might be guilty of bad timing.

"Not at all," Jack assured me. "The sheep can depend on their supply of fat for energy. And if they mate in late August, the ewes drop their lambs in February or March and that's the most favorable time for the lambs to survive. Nature tries to stack the odds in favor of the young, because they are the most vulnerable."

From the lofty heights and canyons of the California bighorn sheep country, I traveled to a desert island in the Great Salt Lake, home for hordes of white pelicans.

"Gunnison Island is the biggest single breeding site for the American white pelican," La Mar Farnsworth, director of Salt Lake City's Hogle Zoo, told me. "Thousands have nested there for as long as we've had reports from the island." Two Air Force helicopters set us down gently on Gunnison, at a spot opposite the major nesting area. With a crew of eight ornithologists and assistants, we had come for the annual pelican roundup of about three dozen young. They are transferred to zoos and laboratories for breeding and research.

"Pelicans must gather in large numbers in order to create a breeding fervor," Mr. Farnsworth said, "and Gunnison Island provides them with a large open space isolated from most predators. However, the adults have to fly a long way to the nearest food source—it's a 50-mile round trip to Bear River Refuge and 160 miles to Utah Lake. But each parent makes the flight daily to feed on freshwater fish; upon its return, it regurgitates food and liquid for the young."

One parent must stay with the eggs or nestlings at all times, for the pelicans are outnumbered about two to one by throngs of shrieking gulls which watch for an unguarded moment to pounce on the nest for a meal. The baby pelicans that live long enough to try their wings are already wise in the ways of survival.

And so, I had found, are most desert animals. Through genetic adaptation and an innate ability to protect themselves from climate and predators, desert creatures —bugs, birds, reptiles, and mammals—thrive in great abundance and diversity.

Mervin Larson, director of the Arizona-Sonora Desert Museum near Tucson, revealed to me—in a way I had never before considered—the vastness of the parade of desert life when he cautioned me once about sleeping directly on the ground. "You only have to look in the morning at all the tracks on a sandy area to realize what a busy place the desert can be on a summer night."

At sunrise the next day, I tested his words and discovered many strange footprints. From then on, I slept on a cot.

Pelican nestlings on Gunnison Island in the Great Salt Lake squawk noisily as trappers gather them for shipment to zoos and laboratories for breeding and study. Thousands of American white pelicans throng the island in spring to nest and raise their young.

Talons splayed, a young red-tailed hawk takes wing after sunning itself at a roadside near Abiquiu, New Mexico.

Swooping to attack, a Cooper's hawk dives at biologist Noel Snyder as he scales a sycamore to inspect the bird's nest and eggs; the helmet helps protect him from beak and talons. Dr. Snyder and his wife, Helen, study the behavior and ecology of hawks in the Southwest and the effects of pesticides on their eggs.

Coyotes *killed by eating fresh meat laced with poison lie rigid in death on Arizona rangeland. The carcass of a horse attracted the scavengers to this bait site. Skull and crossbones (opposite) warn of the presence of other poisoned baits set out by the U. S. Bureau of Sport Fisheries and Wildlife as part of a predator control program designed to protect sheep and cattle grazing on public lands. Stockmen, claiming that coyotes preyed* *heavily on their herds, encouraged the program. But protests and petitions from conservationists and members of humane organizations prompted President Richard M. Nixon in February 1972 to ban the use of poisons for predator control on federal land. The U. S. now permits the killing of the animals by airborne Government riflemen. Coyotes—like the mother and pups at right—prey primarily on rodents and rabbits.*

HAL PERRY, HUMANE SOCIETY OF THE UNITED STATES (ABOVE AND LOWER RIGHT)

DANGER - POISON
DOG OWNERS — TAKE NOTICE
Poisoned Baits in this Area!
DO NOT TAMPER WITH THEM!

POISONED BAITS HAVE BEEN PLACED IN THIS AREA TO CONTROL
ANIMAL DAMAGE TO LIVESTOCK, GAME ANIMALS AND CROPS. YOU
ARE WARNED TO STAY AWAY FROM THESE BAITS, AND TO KEEP
YOUR PETS AWAY. THESE BAITS ARE PROPERTY OF THE U. S.
GOVERNMENT AND ITS OPERATORS.

¡PELIGRO - VENENO!
¡CARNADAS VENENOSAS AQUI!
¡NO LAS TOQUEN!

U.S. DEPARTMENT OF THE INTERIOR
Fish and Wildlife Service · Bureau of Sport Fisheries & Wildlife

Free Spirits, Desert Rats

EVERYONE knows what a desert rat looks like—bewhiskered codger with burro in tow, miner's pick, shovel, and pan tied to the pack saddle. Sure there's gold in those hills, and it's just a matter of making the grubstake last through enough tomorrows to hit pay dirt.

But like much else in our world, the desert-rat field is changing. "One who has lived much on the desert," says Webster's in its broadest definition. And we met artists, rock hounds, antique-bottle collectors, contractors, ex-Marines, and a host of retired folk who had found what they were looking for in the desert life. They are free spirits—desert rats in a larger meaning—and you may call them either; they don't care because they're having too much fun.

Of course, some of the happiest people are those born to that life and content in it without ever having tried any other. Mrs. Kittie Bonner is one, and Lester Valdin is another. I met them both in a onetime silver-bonanza town called Austin, near the geographical heart of Nevada. About a century ago, as many as 10,000 hopeful people moved to the cadences of its mine whistles; now not quite 200 find their hand-me-down town several sizes too big.

"But it's the Lander County seat," Kittie said, "and we try to keep all the county and civic services going, even if there aren't many of us to do it. I served as deputy sheriff for 28 years, and I'm still constable. I've headed the Red Cross for 30 years so that we'll continue to have a chapter in the county."

She sometimes delivers babies. "There's no doctor around here, and some of the Shoshoni Indians depend on me to act as a midwife. Once during a blizzard I delivered a baby in a car out in front of my house when I couldn't persuade the couple to come in. It was about 3 o'clock in the morning, and I only had a flashlight."

In a corner of her living room there was, I noticed, a full-size barber chair. "Yes, I cut hair, too," Kittie said, "but only as a favor to local people, because there's no shop here. And I don't charge for it."

I persuaded her to give me a haircut, and while she worked we talked about the changes in the high basin desert since her childhood. "I was born on an Indian reservation in Oregon in a covered wagon," she said. "Later, we moved to another reservation, and one of my early memories is my aunt playing a small pump organ for the Indians. They brought salmon from the lake and piled it up like cordwood for more music. They thought the organ held a spirit. (Continued on page 168)

Solitude—*the only life for Jim Harrison—holds the 79-year-old trapper to a remote part of northwestern Utah, where he lives in a dugout he built himself. After whittling cottonwood pegs for his traps, he rests in the morning sun; a wood-burning cookstove sits inside the doorway.*

OPUNTIA PHAEACANTHA VAR. MAJOR (UPPER)

Prospector *Frank "Shorty" Harris stretches to his full five-foot height on the baked salt flat of the Devil's Golf Course in Death Valley; short in stature, he stands tall in desert legend. Once when flush he paid a dentist $500 to plate his front teeth and give him a golden smile. That plate proved the only gold he could hang onto; he died penniless in 1934. Shorty profited little from the strikes he claimed, while others grew wealthy by developing them. With a partner in 1904 he made his most famous find—the Bullfrog mine of Nevada. He named it for the shape and greenish color of the first rock discovered containing gold. While drunk, however, Shorty sold his claim for about $1,000. Boom towns such as Rhyolite sprang up briefly near the rich ground, but Shorty moved on. He crossed Death Valley to the Panamint Mountains of California, where with fellow prospector Pete Auguerberry he struck high-grade gold; again he lost his claim. Some prospectors credit him with several discoveries, while others say those who hit pay dirt took pity on him and cut him in for a share. Born in Providence, Rhode Island, in 1856, he worked in cotton mills there before heading west to live the life he described in his own epitaph, that of "a single blanket jackass prospector."*

Vein of silver *lies uncovered behind visitors to a shaft sunk into the Nevada Hills in 1906, the year following the discovery of precious metals. By 1907, the new town of Fairview, Nevada, had 2,000 residents, 27 saloons, and a newspaper. But the land could not provide a profit for all, and after 1908 most of the miners drifted away, the newspaper folded, and silver production fell to 12 percent of the 1907 peak. In 1917, after mining only high-grade ore, the last truly profitable producer closed down.*

Game of pool breaks the monotony of life on a desert ranch in the Pahrump Valley in 1895 for Nevada storekeeper Sam Yount and top-hatted Chief Tecopa. Leader of seven nomadic Paiute Indian bands, Tecopa revealed the location of gold in exchange for food and clothing —such as the top hat and gold-braided bandmaster's uniform he usually wore. He died in his nineties in 1904.

Dream castle in the desolation of Grapevine Canyon in California stands as a monument to flamboyant Death Valley Scotty. With Chicago millionaire Albert M. Johnson, he started building it in 1922 to entertain guests. Today, paying visitors tour the castle, part of Death Valley National Monument.

Running water, music to the ears of any desert veteran, fills a porcelain tub at Scotty's hideaway ranch several miles from the castle. On hot afternoons Scotty liked to laze beneath the spring-fed hose that hangs from a gnarled willow limb. In the castle, water trickling down a panel of multihued native jasper cooled the baronial living room.

Surveying his parched domain in 1918, Death Valley Scotty rides one mule and leads another. Born in Kentucky in the early 1870's, Walter P. Scott moved to Nevada as a boy, worked briefly as a cowhand, then joined a survey team in Death Valley. Later, he spent 12 years with Buffalo Bill's Wild West show and developed a flair for showmanship, a talent many of his cronies said he practiced the rest of his life. He returned to the desert with a grubstake from Johnson and claimed to have discovered a secret mine. Skeptics maintained he "mined" only millionaire Johnson.

Ore cars hold only drifted snow at the Bristol Silver Mine in Nevada, idled in 1971 by dwindling profits; manager Arthur J. Bosch cradles a chunk of malachite copper. Bosch, who started at the Bristol as a miner in the 1940's, stays on to prevent vandalism. If economic conditions improve, the works, 25 miles from Pioche, will reopen. The mine started in 1871 as the National City, but a few

years later a British financier renamed it for his native city. It has produced copper, lead, silver, zinc, and a bit of gold — the only property in the area yielding the first three metals in combination.

"When I was still a little girl, we went to Nevada in four covered wagons. They were coupled together, two and two, and pulled by horses. At times we just went cross-country, without any roads. When it was cold, we put heated stones from our morning fire into burlap bags and put them in the wagon to keep our feet warm. Our whole family came through fine, and we had a canary and a banty hen that hatched a brood on one of our feather beds along the way."

Not only did I get a haircut, but supper as well. I accepted the invitation eagerly because a savory aroma had been coming from a Dutch oven on top of the stove. "Buckaroo chicken," Kittie said as she served. It was while I was on my second helping that Les Valdin dropped by and filled up a plate. As we ate he told me about his prize possession, a Pianola he'd bought more than 20 years ago in Virginia City, Nevada, at the Bucket of Blood Saloon.

"I'd been buckarooing on a ranch up in Oregon and finally got a few days off, so I thought I'd see what Virginia City was like. I went into the Bucket of Blood, and there it was over in the corner, just gathering dust."

Les explained that the Pianola, in a handsome cherrywood cabinet, was a forerunner of the player piano. "When you set it in front of a piano and pump a music roll through it with your feet, a row of padded hammers strikes the keys and plays a tune."

Les loves music—all kinds—and plays violin. "I fell in love with that thing—the Pianola. It worked, and there were about 270 rolls of music for it. I offered the saloonkeeper 175 dollars for it. He said O.K., so we rolled it out to my car, but it wouldn't fit in. So I said it was no deal and went back in for another drink. A little bit later the saloonkeeper came back and said, 'Well, it's all loaded in your car.' I went out, and sure enough it was. But they had to take out the front seat."

Later, I went to Les's place for a recital. For two hours he played, manipulating controls of tempo and loudness to minimize the "rinkitinkiness." There was a Strauss waltz, a bit from "Pagliacci," a Wagnerian interlude. There was "When I Was Twenty-one and You Were Sweet Sixteen," "Salvation Nell," "You Gotta Quit Kickin' My Dog Around." Sounds to dream by, sounds to drink by in the old Bucket of Blood, to toast a sidekick's big strike, to dull the sharp edges of being down and out.

The furnishings of Les Valdin's low-ceilinged room added to my image of this country's rip-snorting past: cavalry swords, Indian arrowheads, a switch lantern from the old Nevada Central Railroad, miners' lamps, shallow gold pans, a pull-down kerosene lamp with a globe of cranberry-red glass, and hanging above the piano in a gold frame the portrait of a Victorian girl with doeish eyes and plunging neckline. "I was told it used to belong to a madam on the Barbary Coast in San Francisco," Les said.

Les collects these things because to him they're the items that history comes wrapped in. "Someday we may want to start a museum here," he explained.

The town of Austin is in fact a living museum of the boom-or-bust days. In 1862 a former pony express rider seeking some strayed horses in a canyon stumbled on a rich silver strike—and the boom was on. Thousands converged, staking every inch, living in shanties, tents, sleeping in the open. Merchants, saloonkeepers, assayers, prostitutes, preachers arrived. For a few years, Austin rivaled the bustle and promise of Virginia City. One Easter Sunday's offering in 1877 raised enough to build and furnish the brick and redwood Episcopal Church, which still serves the town with its original organ and pews.

Les took me to see a landmark of those days, the old stone building that housed the grocery store of R. C. Gridley. Grocer Gridley and a 50-pound sack of flour put Austin on the national map in 1864. "The elections were coming up," Les told me, "and Gridley, who had secessionist leanings, bet on a Democrat for mayor, while a Dr. Herrick, a Union man, bet on the Republican. The loser was to carry a 50-pound sack of flour about a mile and a quarter through the town.

"Gridley lost, and the whole town turned out to see him pay off. The town band marched along with the crowd and played 'John Brown's Body.'

"After Gridley finished the march, he said, 'What'll I do with the flour?' Someone in the crowd said, 'Auction it off,' so he did and said he'd give the money to the Sanitary Fund. That was a fund to help sick and wounded soldiers during the Civil War. The first buyer gave the sack back to be auctioned again. The idea caught on, and before the auctioning stopped, they had raised more than $6,000 for the fund. Virginia City folks heard of it and decided they could do better. So they invited Gridley and his sack of flour to come over, and they reportedly raised better than $25,000. Then came a tour of Nevada and California that raised thousands more and trips back east that brought the total, some people say, above a quarter of a million dollars. That's why I call the story 'Grocer Gridley and his $250,000 Sanitary sack of flour.' "

Up the street from Kittie's porch-shaded adobe-brick house lies a bit of locally historic ground. "That's where the stable was for the camels," Kittie told me.

Camel caravans in Nevada? Yes, and all across the Southwest, in fact. Before he assumed the burden of the Confederate States Presidency, Jefferson Davis, as President Pierce's Secretary of War, had proposed the purchase of camels in the Middle East for Army use in U.S. desert areas. Beginning in the late 1850's, a few surprised Army engineers found themselves in charge of the humped, spitting creatures. Freighters also began to import them, but within a few decades the coming of railroads cut short this experiment in transport.

While the brief era lasted there was an unexpected desert meeting between camels and riverboatmen. In 1857, Captain Alonzo Johnson, who was returning his stern-wheeler down the Colorado River after climbing as far as present-day southern Nevada, sighted Lt. Edward F. Beale driving the first camel train west. The steamboat's whistle frightened the camels, and the camels, strange beasts, greatly mystified the rivermen.

Shallow-draft riverboats, I might add, plied the lower Colorado until about 1910. Paiute Indians learned to gather along the banks where fresh sand bars might ground or wreck the vessels and give them a chance for loot. Captains quickly learned to look for the Indians and evade them.

Though trains could retire the camels and the steamboats, they could never take the place of the burro. Transport for men and goods, burros also on occasion led their owners to silver and gold. The animals would stray from a campsite, and the prospector would make a rich find while hunting them. It happened at Austin, though horses may get the credit there. It happened at Tonopah, Nevada. It happened at Wickenburg, Arizona. It happened in Zane Grey's short story, "Tappan's Burro." It has become one of the West's classic legends.

And to me it seems to say that random prospecting pays off about as well as the systematic kind. Nevada historian Richard G. Lillard writes that accidents of fortune are inevitable in a mineral-rich land: "Many mines have been discovered by pure chance.... A prospector shot at a snake and split a rock of high-grade ore. Three drunken men rolled a boulder down a hill; it chipped off rock and exposed a vein of rich ore. It is said that Henry Comstock found the famous Virginia City lode when he saw queer-looking stuff in a gopher hole.... Guy Pritchard, after failing for years as a prospector, gave up and got a job repairing the old road between Hawthorne and Bodie [California]. After lunch one day he sat down to rest, reached lazily for a rock to throw, and discovered silver and galena worth $90 a ton."

One town's boom might hasten another's bust. Word of a bonanza always started stampedes to the promising new strike, depopulating other communities. Not just the miners went, but the merchants, barmen, good-time girls, and barbers. They piled wagons high with shelving and notions, zinc bathtubs and velvet plush settees, type cases and presses. A prospector hastening into a strange new camp might find himself bending elbows with old friends, being served by the same barman, shaved by the same barber, reading a paper printed on the same press by the same editor he'd left in the waning camp 60 miles back down the road.

I found a historic bar in Rhyolite, Nevada, a ghost town that once teemed with nearly 10,000 people, and now is home to fewer than a dozen. Mrs. Frederica W. Heisler was selling souvenirs across it in her gift shop. The shop occupies what used to be the ladies' waiting room in the still-impressive train station, which Mrs. Heisler inherited from her brother. The tracks have long since been ripped up, and Mrs. Heisler, once a Georgia schoolteacher, lives in the station, collects historical items for her museum in the former men's waiting room, and recites Shakespeare while she sweeps or cooks a meal, for the comforting sound of a human voice, even though it's her own.

"This bar is solid Honduras mahogany," she said, "and when Rhyolite was in its heyday—around 1906—it was on Golden Street, in a saloon called the Club 66. The story goes that the owner chose the name because when he opened for business, he'd invested everything he had except for 66 cents. In the next 20 months more than $300,000 went across that bar.

"I call it the bar where a dead man shot a man dead. See this scar? That's from one of the bullets. A bully provoked a shoot-out in the Club 66 with a much smaller man, and got off the first shot, a mortal wound. But the smaller man had pulled his pistol out of the holster, and just before he fell he squeezed off a shot that killed the bully."

When Rhyolite's bubble burst, the mahogany bar went bouncing by wagon down the road to Beatty, where it supported more elbows and finally ended in storage. There Mrs. Heisler's brother found it and returned it to Rhyolite to be a tangible proof of boisterous years now known only in story.

The stories of the two men who launched Rhyolite's boom by finding the Bullfrog mine have almost become legend: Ed Cross, the partner who invested in a ranch and lived to old age in plenty; Shorty Harris, who, according to his own account, signed away his share for $1,000 and three barrels of whiskey while in an alcoholic haze of celebrating his good fortune. He spent the rest of his life looking for another big strike. Riches eluded him, but somehow he was always able to raise just one more grubstake. Once he parlayed a bag of kittens into a stake, he said, by selling them for $10 apiece in a mining town plagued with rats. William Caruthers, who filled his book *Loafing Along Death Valley Trails* with desert reminiscences, concluded the story in Shorty's words: "One fellow didn't have any money and offered me a goat. I knew a fellow who wanted a goat. . . . Name was Pete Swain.

"Pete was all lit up when I offered him the goat for fifty dollars. He peeled the money off his roll and took the goat into his shack. A few days later Pete came to his door and called me over and shoved a fifty dollar note into my hands. 'I just wanted you to see what that goat's doing,' he said.

". . . The goat was pulling the cork out of a bottle of liquor with his teeth.

" 'That goat's drunk as a boiled owl,' Pete said. 'If I ever needed any proof that there's something in this idea of transmigration of souls, that goat gives it. He's Jimmy, my old sidekick, who I figgered was dead and buried.'

Outdoor living room *gives Ed Yates, 88, a place to rest in the breeze when summer heat settles over Tassi, Arizona. He built his home with local rock and driftwood collected as Lake Mead began to fill behind Hoover Dam in 1938. A spring waters Tassi's 20 acres of pasture, gardens, and cottonwoods. Only two other people live in the town: Yates' daughter Gladys and her husband, Osborne Gentry. But a nearby inlet of the lake draws scattered neighbors who fish for bass, catfish, and crappie, and usually stop at the oasis. Most of the surrounding land remains inhospitable; Grand Wash, just below Tassi, drains hundreds of square miles, and flash floods often follow summer and fall thunderstorms. Gold and silver prospectors have found the region a poor hunting ground; Yates has located unworkable traces of uranium in the area.*

SAM ABELL

Antiques crowd *the living room of Les Valdin's Austin, Nevada, home as he listens to a waltz played on his Pianola. Intrigued by the instrument, he bought it and 267 music rolls from a saloon in Virginia City, Nevada, in the 1940's The bartender removed the front seat of Valdin's car and loaded the Pianola for the drive home. Once a rancher, Valdin still favors a cowboy hat (top).*

Keeping busy *in Austin, Kittie Bonner (above) takes a call beside her begonias. Besides being a prize-winning artist, she has assisted as ambulance attendant on the 92-mile run to the nearest hospital, and still serves as the local midwife and as chairman of the Red Cross chapter. Also a constable and jail matron, she has packed a gun on occasion but never had to use it.*

" 'Now listen,' I said. 'Do you mean to tell me you actually believe that goat is your old pal, whom you drank with and played with and saw buried with your own eyes, right up there on the hill?'

" 'Exactly,' Pete shouted, and he peeled off another fifty and gave it to me. So, you see, a grubstake, like gold, is where you find it."

When Shorty died in 1934, he asked to be buried in Death Valley, beside a friend who had died of exposure there years earlier. Like most prospectors, Shorty was a romantic, even in his epitaph: "Bury me beside Jim Dayton in the valley we loved. Above me write, 'Here lies Shorty Harris, a single blanket jackass prospector.' "

The valley Shorty loved was christened with its dread name by a band of forty niners as they thankfully bade it goodbye. Their passion to dip pans in the gold-rich streams of the Sierra had tempted almost a hundred of them to abandon a proven trail for an unproven shortcut. As a result, they blundered into an ordeal that cost three to eight lives, depending on which account you read. No matter who tells it, the tale is gripping, and it was a favorite of Johnny Mills. I'd heard of Johnny from several old-timers. He had worn himself out in the heat and dust of Death Valley borax diggings and by the 1930's was gardener and yarn-spinner at the luxurious Furnace Creek Inn, which even then was often fully booked months in advance.

Johnny relished getting to the story's climax, when the fear-numbed gold-seekers, desperate for food, water, and some certainty as to where on God's earth they were, got their first forbidding sight of the valley itself. "They came right down Furnace Creek Wash," Johnny emphasized, "right past where you're sittin' now all fed and comfortable."

"But Johnny," ventured a meek little woman, "why in the world did they go through all that? Why didn't they just come and stay at the Furnace Creek Inn?"

"Well, lady," replied Johnny, who didn't like to have his dramatic finish interrupted, "they just hadn't thought to make reservations."

Not all old miners and prospectors had to live on simply their mental replays of yesterday. A few not only struck it big but also managed to hold onto their claims. Perhaps no single spot saw more wealth and high living than Virginia City, Nevada. The town roistered and brawled above the famous Comstock Lode which, unlike most western strikes, not only started rich but ran deep. It yielded both gold and silver, totaling about a half-billion dollars, according to one estimate. Major mine owners became "kings of the Comstock," living with an opulence few monarchs could match. Jerry Lynch rode horses shod with silver, and Mr. and Mrs. Sandy Bowers struck it rich and built a mansion. "Thar ain't no chance for a gentleman to spend his money in this country," said Sandy, so they sailed for Europe "to see the Queen of England and other great men of them countries." Victoria declined to give them an audience, but they cut a lavishly expensive swath across the Continent.

Business was so good that the town never closed. Raw oysters on ice came from San Francisco, and choice California fruits and wines pampered taste buds. Lotta Crabtree's ballet and Edwin Booth's acting put a topping of culture on entertainment that could always fall back on the can-can, the roulette wheel, and whatever spontaneous drunken violence an evening might produce. Below ground another world never closed as miners fought water, crumbling walls, and at times each other in a honeycomb of shafts and tunnels that disgorged bonanza.

On a meanly cold February evening I wound up through junipers and snow

Muted colors, some those of the Arizona desert, shade the art of Ted De Grazia, kneeling in his Gallery in the Sun in Tucson. Here he displays many of his paintings of Mexicans and southwestern Indians — his favorite subjects. Cross sections of cactus stud the central corridor.

patches to the steep east face of Sun Mountain and the storied mining metropolis. A sign on the *Territorial Enterprise* office window invited visitors in to see memorabilia of Mark Twain's literary start—but the door was locked, the inside dark. Just about everything else was closed, too, in the little town, which now booms anew in the summer tourist season. Before the preserved Mackay Mansion, home of a Comstock king, I stopped to admire a patch of grass and shrubs amid the barren gravel and tailings of the hill. A man with a rake smiled a greeting and volunteered, "We have to haul in every bit of soil here if we expect anything to grow."

To me, the old ghost towns seem watchful, waiting for the new strike, another fling at life, like the desert plants and creatures that wait out the bad times for the good—no matter how brief. When good times come, an understandable extravagance rules human behavior. If reality isn't extravagant enough to be entertaining, imagination takes over. And it was Mark Twain's imagination at concocting tales that lifted him above the role of a mere reporter on the *Territorial Enterprise*.

His talents at first were not universally recognized, especially by the rival press. In November 1863 the Austin, Nevada, *Reveille* reported:

"A CANARD.—Some of the papers are expressing astonishment that 'Mark Twain,' the local of the *Territorial Enterprise*, should perpetrate such a 'sell' as 'A Bloody Massacre Near Carson,' a pretended account of [an Indian raid] which recently appeared in the columns of the *Enterprise*. They don't know him. We would not be surprised at *anything* done by that silly idiot."

The *Reveille* itself did its share of hoaxing, however, and its great achievement was the invention—appropriately—of a liars' club. Having become a daily in a typical fit of boomtown euphoria, the paper found news columns hard to fill and turned to pure imagination upon occasion. The result, as I found reported in a delightful little book, *The Town That Died Laughing*, by Oscar Lewis, was the "Sazerac Lying Club." The Sazerac, a local saloon with a clientele of loquacious old-timers, inspired the idea, and a news vacuum at press time launched it thus:

"ELECTED PRESIDENT.—The Sazerac Lying Club was organized last night, our esteemed, prominent, and respected follow-citizen, Mr. George Washington Fibley, being unanimously chosen president of the organization. There was no opposing candidate; his claims and entire fitness for the honorable position being conceded by common consent of the Club."

The *Reveille* next reported that the item had been received with amusement by all the Sazerac's patrons except Mr. Fibley, who had appeared at the office brandishing a cane and demanding an apology. Whereupon, the paper printed:

"APOLOGETIC.—An apology is due from the *Reveille* to Mr. George Washington Fibley. We said in yesterday's issue that he was elected President of the Sazerac Lying Club. This was an error; he was defeated."

The talent for telling it big moved west with the frontier, and it is still prized as an art form among desert people. In Wickenburg, Arizona, I stopped to visit William G. (Bill) Bass, to see some of his excellent wildlife movies and hear about his early days roving the Grand Canyon. That great chasm was his boyhood classroom, for his father William Wallace Bass raised a family there while building trails and leading the first tourist parties across to the North Rim on burros. When I asked about tall tales, Bill mentioned the legend that a single drink from Wickenburg's Hassayampa River renders a man immune to the truth forever. Then he said:

"Once when I was walking down by the Colorado River, the fish were jumping up, just asking to be caught, but I hadn't brought any fishing gear. So I looked around and cut me a pole from an ocotillo and made myself a line from some yucca fiber. I cut myself a hook from a fishhook cactus. But I didn't have any bait.

"About that time I looked down and saw a snake with a lizard in its mouth. Now I always carried a little 'snake bite medicine' with me, so I just poured a few drops into the snake's mouth and he let go of the lizard. I put the lizard on my hook and right away I caught a fish.

"But I wanted to catch another one, and so I looked down for more bait and, do you know, there was that same snake waiting with another lizard in his mouth."

By the turn of the century, there had arisen the image of the grizzled old desert prospector who has really found the big one and could spend in a grand manner. Walter P. Scott was a man prepared from youth to play that role, and he was never bested. To the world he was the fabulous Death Valley Scotty.

At Scotty's Castle, a miragelike multimillion-dollar monument to his imagination, I paused before a painting that had been one of his favorites. It showed a cowboy riding his mount right into a saloon, six-guns blazing holes in the ceiling, scattering patrons, to the dismay of some and amusement of others. Here was the wild moment Scotty loved, and he lived such moments as often as he could and filled in the boring spots with mental extravaganzas. He called it "whoop-de-doodle."

By age 10 Scotty had left an unhappy homelife in Kentucky for the mining towns of Nevada. He worked with a desert survey party and mule team drivers, learned the cowboy's lonely life in Wyoming, and by the time he was 18 had become a trick rider with Buffalo Bill Cody's Wild West show. For the next 12 years he toured America and Europe, met the Prince of Wales in England, gaped at castles in Spain, and learned to admire the Cody brand of flamboyant showmanship.

When he left the show he headed for Death Valley, an area that had stuck in his mind since his surveying days. Fitted out as a prospector, he vanished into the desert. Here the legends increasingly get the better of the facts.

The castle is fact enough—battlemented towers crown cream-stucco walls and Spanish red-tile roofs, and ornately carved wood gates guard arching entrances; inside stretches a progression of 15 richly furnished rooms, including a regal music chamber with grand piano and huge pipe organ rigged to play duets from perforated rolls. We spent an afternoon and star-bright evening there—my wife and sons and I—talking of the mixture of fact and fiction that was Scotty's life.

In 1904 Scotty reappeared out of the desert, throwing around great amounts of money. He hired a whole Santa Fe train to run him to Chicago from Los Angeles in a record 44 hours, 54 minutes. According to Scotty, he did it to promote railroad stocks, and he plunked down "a hundred grand" before an incredulous Santa Fe official and said, "I want to leave Sunday at one." Another version holds that it was all a publicity stunt dreamed up by an imaginative reporter who promoted the financing without Scotty's being out a penny. Whatever the truth, headlines announced the train's race with time, and plain Walter Scott quickly became Death Valley Scotty, a national celebrity.

People thought a secret mine explained his sprees—silver dollars flung to scrambling crowds, waiters tipped with $20 banknotes clipped from mint-fresh rolls. Enjoying it all was Albert M. Johnson, Chicago millionaire, who seemed to be having much to do with building the great house that began in 1922 to rise in Death Valley's Grapevine Canyon. But the place was called Scotty's Castle.

A will and the deed to the castle became public after Johnson's death in 1948, and Scotty's name appeared on neither. The castle passed to the Gospel Foundation, a creation of Johnson's, and in 1970 became an addition to Death Valley National Monument. Scotty's death in 1954 revealed no secret mine.

But the house continues to be called Scotty's Castle, and I feel sure that's how Johnson would have wanted it. He credited Scotty with persuading him to come west and strive for lost health after being told by doctors to find a warm climate. As it turned out, that decision bought him 42 years more of life, including many good times hearing Scotty relive his varying versions of the past.

"I remember one time I was out on the desert," Scotty would begin, and his audience, in winter around the huge fireplace in the baronial main hall, in summer under the stars at the courtyard fountain, would lean forward expectantly. White Stetson pushed back on a shock of white hair, blue eyes crinkling, stout form slouching comfortably, he held his hearers captive: "I found a man and woman almost dead. They were so weak that it would kill them to try to take them in. But I was out of food, and they would die before I could get back with some. I had me a real problem." And here he would pause.

"Gracious, Mr. Scotty, what did you do?"

"There was only one thing to do, ma'am—I had to shoot 'em."

And then, amid the initial stunned silence and the mounting laughter as his listeners realized he had taken them in, he'd make his exit. He usually spent the night at "the lower ranch," a three-room cabin several miles away. Scotty much preferred it to the castle.

Once as he sat by the fountain, he gazed up at a rounded, barren hill above the castle and remarked, "When I pass on, that's where I'd like to be buried. I'd keep dry and cool up there."

Today the hill wears a cross above the graves of Scotty and a favorite dog Windy. The castle lives on as in his lifetime, only busier because hundreds of visitors file through it every day. On the roof above them black metal weathervanes, each a silhouette of a prospector, shift with every change of wind, like gold seekers whipped this way and that by the latest rumors.

I came too late to Death Valley to encounter any of the old skinners who once drove the Borax Company's famed 20-mule teams from Furnace Creek to the railhead at Mojave, 165 miles away. But I did find a man who'd been a swamper and skinner with mule trains about the turn of the century. And R. A. (Cap) Gibson, now in his eighties, looked like part of the old West with his trim Buffalo Bill mustache and beard, brown Stetson and boots, and leather riding pants.

"When you take a job as a swamper," he told me, "you trade your blanket for a lantern. The swamper has to roll out before anyone else to feed and harness the mules, start a fire, cook breakfast. The skinner's a king and has a pretty good life, but the swamper has to wait on everybody, including the mules."

The original teams—actually 18 mules and 2 horses—pulled two heavy wagons in tandem, each loaded with 24,000 pounds of borax, plus a 1,200-gallon water tank—up to 73,200 pounds in all! When the mules turned a corner, they exerted such an inward pull that the wagons would have left the road but for some special acrobatics by three pairs of mules. They were trained to jump over the chain that ran the length of the train and pull against the turn to keep the wagons on the right track. From 1883 to 1888, the mule trains ran year round without a single breakdown across some of the world's worst terrain—below-sea-level salt flats, desolate mountains, and a great sweep of the Mojave Desert.

Though Cap Gibson's experience was with 16-mule teams, it was still a tricky business. "I remember once we had new mules that were untrained. Every mule has to get used to being in a certain order in the team, and once you train him, he won't want to be any place else. But these mules hadn't yet been trained to work in any spot. We started trying to hitch them up at five in the morning, and it was three in the afternoon before we had them harnessed in spans. The next morning we did better. We had them in harness and ready by ten.

Horse rancher Hube Yates, 69, tends his mounts at dawn in the corral of his Walnut Castoria Ranch high on the mountainous Mogollon Rim near Heber, Arizona. During the winter, he operates a riding concession for the Carefree Inn near Carefree, a desert town 195 miles to the southwest. He takes about 11 days for the fall and spring trail drives between the town and the ranch he bought 22 years ago to escape the heat of summer. A horseman all of his life, Yates broke and trained the 15 animals in his string. He came to Arizona at 11 when his family moved from Oklahoma in two covered wagons.

Yellowing posters peel from an office wall (above) of the old Eureka Sentinel, *a newspaper founded in Eureka, Nevada, in 1872. Other handbills — reporting events ranging from boxing matches to murder — line the pressroom where publishers Don and Linda Critchell (opposite) study an edition of their* Eureka Miner, *a weekly newspaper they started in 1971 with 479 subscribers. That year they bought the Sentinel* Building, planning to restore it as a working museum. But after printing just 29 issues there, a leaking roof and chill winter weather prompted them to move into a trailer and let the building revert to its former owners. They now print most of the paper on the press of the Ely Daily Times, 78 miles to the east. The state of Nevada has declared the Sentinel Building a historic monument, and the Critchells still hope to see it restored.

"That was some trip. About the time we got the mules tamed down we hit a blizzard in Cajon Pass and had to hole up at a vacant ranch. When we got to the Mojave River, it was running high because of the storm. We had to get across, and so when a local man showed us a good ford, we plunged right in, with me on the seat throwing stones at any mule that looked like he had ideas of slowing up. We went across like we were on a bridge. Next day we broke camp for Death Valley."

Men who would take on the desert would often take on the law if it got in their way. The big country and spotty enforcement often encouraged a desperate man. Nevada killer Sam Brown walked Genoa streets with impunity until he tried to shoot down innkeeper Henry Van Sickles. To protect himself, Henry ambushed Sam and killed him with a shotgun. A coroner's jury ruled that Sam "has come to his death from a just dispensation of an all-wise Providence. It served him right."

In eastern Utah I crossed and recrossed an outlaw trail that once stretched from Hole-in-the-Wall, a desperadoes' redoubt in Wyoming, all the way to Mexico. Along it wanted men shifted locales as prudence dictated. Butch Cassidy and his Wild Bunch found a remote hideout at the edge of the San Rafael Desert in Utah, where a maze of canyons guarded the approach. "The Robbers' Roost" today lies on the ranch of Art Ekker, who took me there and pointed out landmarks: "That little rock down there, we call him Butch. . . . Here's Silvertip Spring. . . . the gang would hole up in this draw and post their lookouts on the rocks above."

Butch's baggage-car robberies so provoked the Union Pacific that it recruited its own forces to pursue him. He eluded them, however, and was gunned down with the Sundance Kid in a one-sided clash with a Bolivian Army unit in South America. "There are accounts that they didn't really get him, that he came back to this country and died of old age," Art said.

Desert legends abound, and the most tantalizing of them—the tales of buried treasures and lost mines—persist and grow year after year. In Nevada we heard of the Lost Chicken Craw, in Death Valley the Lost Chinaman; Arizona has its Lost Treasure of Cochise, and many areas have a Lost Treasure of Montezuma. Almost everywhere we heard stories of robbers fleeing so fast from the law that they hastily buried their loot or stowed it in some cave, never to find it again. Each season brings new crops of "clues" that send new crops of fortune-seekers into the wilds.

The lost-mine story is almost a classic stereotype: An old-timer makes a rich discovery of ore, but he can never find his way back to it. Indians cause him to flee before he can get his bearings, or heat and exposure addle his brain, or a deluge sweeps away landmarks. But he and others, invited or uninvited, never quit the search. The Lost Breyfogle fits this pattern. In 1863 Charles Breyfogle found rich ore while fleeing Indians near Death Valley, but the ordeal robbed him of his bearings, and though he tried for years, he never made his way back. But he did add a word to the language for those who futilely seek such mines—Breyfoglers.

I never got much interested in looking for mines until I met Hubert Ammon Yates. Now he's stirred my curiosity about the fabled Lost Dutchman, said to lie somewhere east of Phoenix, Arizona, in the Superstition Mountains. Not that Hube's interested in finding it—his overwhelming interest is horses. But he thinks he knows where the Lost Dutchman is.

As a boy Hube helped handle the teams as his family moved west from Oklahoma in covered wagons. "As we got out to Arizona, I remember passing cavalry still stationed here to keep an eye on the Indians," he told me. He's always worked with horses, and in winter he handles trail rides for the Carefree Inn at Carefree, Arizona. In summer he and his family move to cooler quarters among the ponderosa pines atop the Mogollon Rim. They do it in the old-fashioned way, riding and driving their string of horses 195 miles across desert and mountains. In fall they make the trip back to Carefree. It's an 11-day test of riding and stamina each way, and Hube has done it for 22 years. A few paying riders go along, to test their horsemanship, see the country, and enjoy Hube's stories.

A favorite is about a drunk who asked Hube to roll him a cigarette. Hube, who neither drinks nor smokes, gave it his best but spilled so much tobacco that he was asked to stop: "Forget it. I didn't know you was drunk, too."

A big man, over six feet, Hube has two sons and at least one grandson bigger than he is. He hides an affection for his herd with brusque talk. "There's a hell for horses, too, you know," he says to one that's acting up. Of another, "That horse has three gaits—trot, stumble, and fall." And of a wild one he was trying to break, "When that horse went up, you could see sunlight on his belly."

But about the Lost Dutchman, Hube explained that years ago he'd befriended a man who claimed to have learned the secret from the "Dutchman" himself, a German named Jacob Waltz. The friend later confided in Hube.

We talked about the legion of tales that had arisen around Old Jake and his mine, until the fiction has drowned the fact. "I've heard stories about that treasure ever since I hit Arizona," Hube said.

Legend says Apaches, or perhaps Pimas, found the gold first. Then Don Miguel Peralta de Córdoba became Spanish owner of the Superstition Mountains through a royal land grant, and three sons supposedly found the mine. Versions of how it happened vary widely. I like the one that has a Peralta daughter romantically involved with a man named Carlos. The affair outraged the father, who sent a tracker after the fleeing Carlos, and the tracker stumbled upon the gold.

Old Jake entered the picture in the 1870's, after Arizona passed from Spanish to Mexican to American hands. Only he was young Jake then, with his friend from boyhood days in Germany, Jacob Weiser. They somehow learned the secret of the Peralta mine—at least they began paying for all their purchases from pouches heavy with gold dust and nuggets. There are many accounts of how they got the mine. One story says they saved the life of a Peralta heir after he'd been wounded in a gambling quarrel. In gratitude, the young man shared the mine's wealth with them and eventually deeded over the mine itself. Another version has Jake out alone in the Superstitions, coming upon three Mexicans helping themselves to the mine's vast wealth, and Jake shooting the three in cold blood to acquire possession.

"He's supposed to have shot other men, too—the ones that tried to trail him to his mine," Hube said. There's disagreement on how many Jake put away in his supposed private cemetery in the Superstitions; the counts run as high as eight, including his friend Jacob Weiser. But other stories say Indians killed Weiser.

Old Jake finally died in 1891, and the mine has been sought by a succession of men ever since, including a territorial governor, A. P. K. Stafford. At least one searcher as late as 1931 met death; Adolph Ruth reportedly was found with two bullets in his head after being missing six months among the rugged peaks. "Some people spend their whole lives looking for these lost mines," Hube said. "That's not for me. I've got everything I want with my horses and family and friends. I don't have any use for a mine.

"But I think I could go there. When you start getting close to it, there's the name 'Teddy Roosevelt' on a rock, and the reason nobody's found it yet is. . . ."

I'll give no more details. I still have hopes that someday Hube and I can go looking for the Dutchman. And I've already renounced any interest in getting rich. Wealth would leave me with no reason to poke around the desert looking for things. A desert rat can put himself right out of business if he's not careful.

Walking staff *in hand, author and backpacker Colin Fletcher (above) strides through the pale scrub of Last Chance Canyon, near Death Valley. In 1958, at age 36, he hiked the length of California in six months. He later chronicled the trek in his first book,* The Thousand-Mile Summer.

Embarking *on a journey through the Grand Canyon, hiker Harvey Butchart pauses at Enfilade Point to gaze at the Colorado River far below. A professor of mathematics at Northern Arizona University in Flagstaff, Dr. Butchart has walked 15,000 miles in the Canyon in about 20 years. "It's intellectual curiosity and the lure of overcoming danger that keeps me at it," he says.*

The Desert Today And Tomorrow

TO THOSE WHO'VE LIVED WITH IT—for a day or a lifetime—it's simply "the road," and either they love it or hate it, for its axle-breaking rocks and eye-stretching blue distances leave little room for neutrality. "The road" is Baja California's Highway 1, which winds a thousand miles from the peninsula's northern boundary to its southern tip. When we traveled it, 360 miles still remained an unpaved, body-wrenching endurance test of pot holes and ruts, sharp turns, steep grades, and deep sands. Along its most punishing sections, derelict cars and trucks lay abandoned where they failed, cannibalized for parts to rescue other vehicles.

Motorists defeated by the road's hazards can expect to be rescued too. "Anyone who has ever needed help out here becomes a good Samaritan for life," said a truck driver I met along the way. Not long after, we had the opportunity to offer aid to a young man bending over the engine of a vintage car with a dead battery. When we stopped, his response startled us. He shot his right arm through our open window and vigorously honked the horn. Then he thanked us and explained, "My companions will hear and remember to come back. They left two hours ago to get help at a rancho not far down the road." His abrupt action fitted the pattern of the young people we met in the peninsula's desert country—direct but courteous.

The road, though it breaks machines, builds character, I've decided. But today it's vanishing fast; perhaps a hundred miles more will be paved by the end of 1972. Before long, the smooth, winding ribbon, advancing from both north and south, will meet, and most Baja Californians look forward to the day.

"We want the paved road," said Becky Carillo, with whom we stayed in San Ignacio. "People would like to be able to drive to the next town without getting jolted and coated with dust. Besides, the pavement will bring lots of tourists."

Remoteness from markets and scarcity of water limit farming and industry, and many of the 600,000 or so peninsula residents look elsewhere for an exploitable resource—to tourism. On San Quintín Bay, at a sportsman's retreat called the Old Mill, manager Alfonso Vela spoke of big real estate promotions already under way along the arterial highway and predicted boom times: "The sleeping giant will awaken. Baja California will really be something."

While many in Baja California hope to prosper from tourism, Arizonans have already made their state a mecca for people and industry. Dr. Daniel E. Noble, chairman, Motorola Science Advisory Board, *(Continued on page 192)*

Early-morning sun *lights the faces of Mennonite boys on a farm near Nuevo Casas Grandes. Their grandfathers came to the area from Canada in the 1920's. "We love the open spaces here," one farmer said. "Mexico has been a land like few others for our children."*
YUCCA SP. (UPPER); SAM ABELL (OPPOSITE)

Mennonite farmer unloads milk cans from a wagon at a cheese factory in Capolin, Chihuahua. Straining the milk through a cloth, Abram Neufeld (opposite) completes the first stage in processing queso menonita—Mennonite cheese. His father Cornelius leans over steel containers filled with chunks of cheese ready for compression and shipment to markets throughout Mexico.

Capolin, a colony of a thousand, herds 2,500 head of cattle on land watered by wells, some as deep as 750 feet. Well pumps run on gas, since Old Colony Mennonites of Mexico reject electricity. Firm believers that God wants them to till the soil, they raise their own grains and fruit. Women wear homemade clothing exclusively; men now buy their overalls in neighboring towns.

Weathered stone and wooden crosses stand in the cemetery below Terlingua in the Big Bend country of west Texas. Untended graves rest above ground on barren limestone. During the first half of the 20th century, quicksilver mining brought prosperity to remote Terlingua. Dwindling markets closed down the mines in the 1940's. Amid the town's crumbling ruins stands the small, abandoned Church of Santa Inés (right). There in October 1971 Father Joe Hermoso officiated at the first wedding in the church in a quarter of a century; Paul Gonzales and his bride Virginia Benavidez kneel at the altar.

N.G.S. PHOTOGRAPHER JAMES L. STANFIELD (UPPER)

recognized Arizona's special assets in 1947, when he was setting up a Motorola electronics laboratory. Dr. Noble explained why he had chosen Phoenix as the site for the first plant: "We were in competition for scientists and engineers, and we thought this place would attract them, and it did. I'm sure people joined us partly because they looked forward to living in Arizona." Since then some 850 firms have settled around Phoenix, many of them part of the state's thriving electronics industry.

In nearby Scottsdale, former Mayor Morton E. Kimsey, 83, has seen his community grow from a small cowtown to a plush resort. Population soared from 743 in 1940 to more than 70,000 in 1972, and it is still growing. "Lots of boys were stationed around here during World War II, and after the war many returned to stay," explained Mr. Kimsey. "Then a flood of tourists arrived, some of them suffering from asthma or arthritis. Often they became permanent residents."

But not everyone is rejoicing. George H. Thomas, 71, who has lived all his life in Scottsdale, complained that the people who have moved in have covered with houses and apartments what was once "a pretty decent place."

Tucson has grown so much that astronomers there find the increased sky glow from the city interfering with their work. They chose the area partly because of the clear air and the frequency of cloudless nights. But Tucson, a town of 45,000 in 1950, is home now to 263,000, and it lights up the night sky over 80 square miles. A city ordinance limits outdoor lighting, but, as Dr. Arthur A. Hoag, of Kitt Peak National Observatory, put it, "Tucson will not grow dimmer, for as the city expands, it will become brighter. The new ordinance simply slows the pace."

While bright lights plague astronomers, smoke from copper smelters, factories, and power plants has in places blurred the clarity of the desert air. Thus the arid regions, as well as the rest of the country, have begun to pay the price of progress and development—the pollution of the air, water, and land.

So there are two sides to change in the desert. There are those who share the view reported by Joseph Wood Krutch that Baja California is "a splendid example of what bad roads can do for a country. It must be almost as beautiful as it was when the first white man saw it in 1533." And there is the frontiersman's urge to tame the land—to master it before it masters him.

"The harshness of the desert has been its best protection in the past," said historian Sid Brinckerhoff. "But now man no longer feels its savagery. He has air conditioning and all kinds of vehicles to span the distances. Before the days of four-wheel drive you were lucky if you could get off the main road and survive."

Now as people see deserts eaten away by new housing and industrial parks and interstate highways, they worry increasingly about ways to keep some portions untamed for future generations.

We found one example of the positive approach to conservation at the new Guadalupe Mountains National Park 110 miles east of El Paso in the Chihuahuan Desert. There officials are contemplating a novel concept of park use and protection, including a ride by aerial tramway to the lofty lip of a limestone cliff. Visitors would also stroll trails that afford views of pristine forest—home of elk, deer, bear, and mountain lion—and far-horizon panoramas of the lower desert.

"We're seeking a way to allow people to appreciate the fragile ecosystems without destroying them," Donald A. Dayton told me. Superintendent of Carlsbad Caverns National Park, just to the north in New Mexico, he also heads the staff at the 76,306-acre Guadalupe Park in Texas. "We have a unique forest up in The Bowl, above 8,000 feet. Species of trees there are really left over from the Ice Age. Douglas fir, aspen, and pines once grew over much of this country, but now you find these in this area only on lofty 'islands' (Continued on page 198)

NOTICE
NO GAS-FOOD OR LODGING NEXT 120 MILES

SHADED PARKING AREA FOR CARS WITH PETS

← 7 FT. CLEARANCE

Roadside signs *greet desert travelers, cautioning motorists to fill up near Mimbres, New Mexico, and directing pet owners at Hoover Dam on the Colo-* *rado River. The Mojave Desert Soil Conservation District warns against land abuse near Shoshone, Nevada. Wedding chapels share billboards with* *restaurants outside Las Vegas. A Reno "Waffle & Pie Ranch" advertises fresh orange juice, and another establishment offers weddings on credit.*

It's **your** desert
enjoy and use it
don't abuse it
Or You will Lose it !

MOJAVE DESERT SOIL CONSERVATION DISTRICT

he **TEXAN'S**

WAFFLE & PIE RANCH

E. 9th St

WE SQUEEZE NAVELS 630 TO 12

GETTING *Married*?
LAS VEGAS WEDDING CENER

Potato Pancakes & BLINTZES

Chapel
MINISTER J.P. PHOTOS
Flowers and Rings

PASTRAMI or PIE

St. Francis

4 hrs. PARKING 50

Wedding Bells Chapel
MARRIAGE LICENSE
INFORMATION

All Approved CREDIT CARDS Welcome Here.

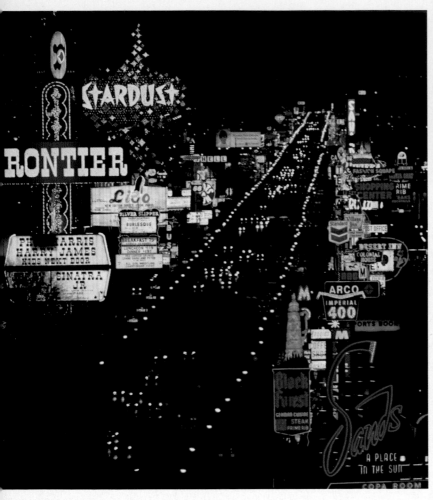

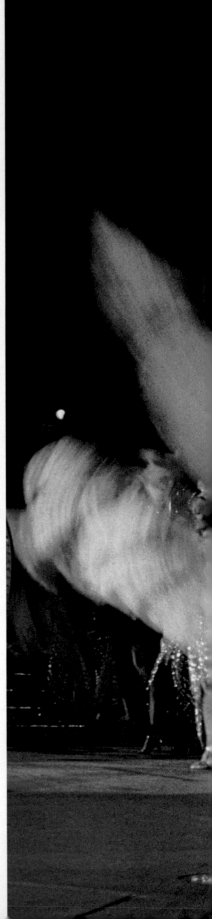

Neon corridor—the famed Las Vegas "Strip"—entices visitors to the "Entertainment Capital of the World." The city welcomes more than 15 million visitors annually to nightclubs and casinos. In 1971 gaming tables and slot machines by the thousand took in nearly 400 million dollars in gross taxable revenue.

Sequins glitter as dancers in the lavish Lido de Paris revue perform at the Stardust, a large resort hotel. Other million-dollar productions—the Folies Bergere and Casino de Paris—also dazzle Las Vegas audiences.

in the desert mountains. Scientists are very interested in the Guadalupe vegetation in the highlands and in the unusual assemblage of plants and animals."

That's why the proposed master plan includes no roads to the high country. "We won't even take packhorses into the forest," Don Dayton said, "because of the possibility of overgrazing, trampling, and introducing seeds from foreign plants. We're trying to preserve this area as a living laboratory."

On the other hand, a report by the U. S. Bureau of Land Management indicates that Californians are loving their deserts to death. For the urban population of southern California the desert offers open spaces that refresh the spirit. Campers, hikers, picnickers, hunters, rock hounds, dune-buggy drivers, sailplaners, sand-chariot sailors, and trail-bike riders find adventure and recreation in the desert. But the Bureau of Land Management warns, ". . . the things that give the desert its appeal—fragile flowers, unique wildlife, ancient relics . . . and a sense of untouched open space—these values are in peril, and we may indeed run out." The report urgently pleads for preservation of desert resources.

In the view of Dr. Aden Baker Meinel and his wife Marjorie, of the University of Arizona's Optical Science Center, the desert's greatest resource is sunlight. They are working on ways to put it to work to produce low-cost electricity without pollution. "We believe the Nation can obtain a significant amount of its power needs from solar energy within 20 years," Dr. Meinel said.

The Meinels' system envisions fields of energy-gathering plates in the sun-drenched desert. An array of plates assembled in 20-foot widths and supported by posts would stretch for hundreds of feet, positioned so the ground beneath would still receive enough sun to support whatever life the moisture would normally sustain. Nitrogen-filled tubing within the plates would absorb heat to near 1,000° F. and pipe it to reservoirs—huge tanks of molten salts. The reservoirs would provide steam for powering turbines to drive generators.

Putting the sun to work also figures in a scheme developed by Carl N. Hodges and his colleagues at the University of Arizona's Environmental Research Laboratory. "Some time ago I became interested in the problem of life along desert sea-coasts," said Mr. Hodges. "People need water, food, and electric power, and we've developed a technology that integrates and provides all three."

I saw his concept brought to life above a barren sweep of beach beside the Gulf of California, at Puerto Peñasco in Sonora. Beneath twin distilling towers of the desalinization plant stood a diesel electric-generating station and four blimp-like, air-supported plastic greenhouses.

"It was the waste heat off the power plant that started me thinking about the concept," Mr. Hodges said. "I hated to see the energy get lost." So he and his staff developed ways to use the heat in the distilling of sea water to nourish vegetables. Next came the idea for air-supported greenhouses, more economical than those held up by rigid frames. Finally, moisture was added to the greenhouse atmosphere by circulating air through asbestos honeycombs moistened by sea water; this minimized the amount of fresh water needed by the roots.

When I stepped through an airlock to enter one of the plastic enclosures, I was struck by the abrupt change. It was like being spirited to an equatorial rain forest. I walked between vibrant leafy columns of green that seemed twice my height. They turned out to be stringbeans—and I felt like Jack getting his first view of the beanstalk. Agustin Cortes, who helps run the University of Arizona-University of Sonora facility, explained, "We grow bumper crops of just about any garden vegetable—broccoli, lettuce, beets, spinach, melons. We don't use sprays because we don't have any insects. When a plant needs pollinating, we do it by hand."

A Tucson firm, Environmental Farms, Inc., is expanding its greenhouses to a ten-acre production unit that aims for an annual harvest of four million pounds of tomatoes, and as Agustin Cortes pointed out, "With never a worm in a tomato."

In California's Imperial Valley we found a place where worms would be a tidbit rather than a menace. We visited the Mesquite Lake Catfish Farm near Brawley.

"But why a catfish farm in the desert?" I asked Robert Dailey, then the manager.

"Catfish like warm water—a temperature of 85 degrees is optimum. In fact they thrive in it," Bob replied. "And the soil in this immediate area is a sand-free caliche, impervious to water and bad for farming. It's perfect for our ponds, because we don't lose any water to seepage. In the summer, though, we lose a lot to evaporation —about three to four million gallons a day."

The day I visited the farm, Bob and his sons were filling crates with alternate layers of ice and catfish for an order from a San Diego seafood restaurant. As he worked he described one of those typical desert-country extravaganzas. Every year on the Fourth of July he floats down the Colorado River along with about 1,200 other people, all in inner tubes. The race starts at Laguna Dam and continues for 15 arm-flailing miles to Yuma, Arizona. Bob takes a special interest in the event— he's a three-time winner in the over-35 class.

I've never tried riding an inner tube in the Colorado, but I have ridden a trail bike high above it. Smaller and lighter than a motorcycle, a trail bike is geared for rough terrain. Its wheels can leave scars that invite erosion, and it draws the dis-approving frowns of many conservationists. But Dick Wilson of Moab, Utah, is a trail-bike enthusiast as well as a conservationist, and he's found a solution.

"Above Moab there's a big area of red Navajo sandstone that once was sand dunes," Dick told me. "It has a slickrock surface, bare of vegetation and with excellent traction, like sandpaper. The expanse of stone is still as undulating as the old dunes. It's great for trail-bike riding, and you can never wear it out."

Dick surveyed a route and persuaded the Bureau of Land Management to authorize the 15-mile Moab Slickrock Bike Trail. He let me try a brief solo on his Honda Trail 90, and I roller-coastered among high swells of sandstone above the Colorado River.

Dick Wilson recognizes the special assets of desert country and tries to work with them. He and many others I met were following a philosophy expounded to me by Dr. Paul B. Sears, former director of Yale University Conservation Program, whom I visited in Taos, New Mexico. "As an ecologist it's my duty to try to see the whole picture," he said, "and this tells me that the desert has had about all it can take of people who are in one way or another intent on tearing it up. We need more people intent on working with nature, not against her."

At Las Cruces, New Mexico, I found such a person. Dr. Carlton Herbel of the United States Department of Agriculture took me to the nearby Jornada Experimental Range on the northern fringe of the Chihuahuan Desert. This rolling area above the Rio Grande once lay under a mat of grasses so thick in places you could harvest hay. Then stockmen brought in cattle, which ate mesquite beans as well as grass, and spread the shrub. In the competition for water, the grasses lost. Over-grazing and recurrent drought speeded the decline of the range, and the bare soil between the clumps of mesquite eroded away.

Now the USDA has found ways to eliminate mesquite, and the range is making a comeback. "We've used planes to spray a herbicide that kills mesquite only," Dr. Herbel said. His hand swept a rolling area of wind-rippled grasses, now straw-yellow in the November sun. "A lot of land in west Texas, southern New Mexico, Nevada, and southeast Arizona is also being treated this way," he added. "We're producing grass on land that ranchers went broke on."

At the Jornada range, and at sites in the Great Basin, Sonoran, and Mojave Deserts, more than 100 investigators are gathering and compiling information on the fragile desert environment. Scientists are studying every facet of life, climate, soil, and water; they feed their findings into computers to create a mathematical model of the desert. "For example," said Dr. James MacMahon, assistant director of the Desert Biome Study centered at Utah State University, Logan, "we are trying to determine what role rodents really play in the deterioration of rangelands. The rodent may be competing with the cow for food, but how important, we wonder, is the rodent in pruning back shrubs and stimulating new growth. What are the positive effects of aerating the soil and taking seeds down to burrows where they germinate more readily?"

Dr. MacMahon's enthusiasm revealed his intense interest: "We need to find ways to make the systems in nature more productive; we need to develop alternatives to the classical approach to desert agriculture; we need to develop a technology that permits us to use the desert without importing water."

Glen Canyon Dam on the Colorado had collected water "imported" from the Rockies to create a new lake straddling the Utah-Arizona border. To farmers Lake Powell represents irrigation and flood control. To others it means electric power, recreation, and beauty. To still others it demonstrates how the works of man can drown natural splendors. For river rats, too, it is a sad monument because high water no longer purges downstream campsites of last year's footprints and beer cans, and no longer piles banks with clean driftwood for cookfires.

We had sad feelings about Lake Powell, because its 186-mile length has covered a sandstone-walled fantasia called Glen Canyon. But then we took a five-day cruise on the lake, and we found an incredibly beautiful world of sky-blue water, red-rock cliffs, and labyrinthine canyons.

Our friend Ted Ekker, whose 18-foot power boat was our ark on this desert lake, had many reasons to mourn the loss of Glen Canyon, for part of his boyhood world had vanished beneath the waters.

"The Chaffin Ranch used to be there," Ted remarked as we passed the mouth of Trachyte Creek. "When I was young, our whole family would come here to pick and can peaches from the orchard. The roads were so rough we couldn't get the ripe peaches home to can them. While we were at Chaffin's we'd also catch fish in the river and salt them. It was like a holiday."

We floated high above the old streambed where a big dredge once dug and washed the sands looking for gold, then nosed into side chasms so narrow and over-hung with rock that noonday was like twilight. Ted inched our boat to within a quarter-mile of 309-foot-high Rainbow Bridge where, according to Navajo legend, visitors may leave their cares forever.

Through it all we followed Ted's example of scooping up clear, cold lake water whenever we felt thirsty. We trusted his lifelong experience with Colorado River water, and we thrived on it.

"Wouldn't it be wonderful," Virginia mused one evening, "if our sons could bring their children here one day and still find water pure enough to drink?"

And if enough of us learn in time to work with the desert and not against it, perhaps it can be so.

Palm Springs, *a California resort and retirement community, brushes the edge of the Sonoran Desert. Beyond the town, the San Gorgonio Pass provides access through the San Jacinto Mountains—and funnels smog from the Los Angeles area. In the 1880's, a San Francisco attorney built a home and an irrigation canal here to create an oasis of fruit trees and vineyards. Today's population of 22,500 more than triples on winter weekends; many vacationists come to play the area's 30 golf courses.*

Cattlemen Fred and Cliff Wood ford a creek on the 15,000-acre ranch they once owned in Aravaipa Canyon, Arizona. Fred (left) named the point behind them Hell's Half Acre. "For many years my brother and I realized our ranch was outstanding in its unique beauty," Fred says. "With our love for it we wanted to preserve it for all to enjoy. It took us over four years to find a group—The Nature Conservancy in Washington, D.C.— that would buy it and not subdivide it."

Rising level of man-made Lake Powell inundates the Cathedral in the Desert in southern Utah. Impounded waters of the Colorado River and its tributaries now almost cover this sandstone formation. The new lake, 186 miles long, provides a source of hydroelectric power, helps assure a continuous flow of water downstream, and serves as a reservoir and national recreation area.

Illustrations and illustrations references appear in *italics*.

Acknowledgments

The Special Publications Division is grateful to the individuals and organizations listed here for their generous cooperation and assistance during the preparation of this book:

Arizona-Sonora Desert Museum; Lyman Benson, Chairman, Department of Botany, Pomona College; Everett L. Cooley, Curator, Western Americana, University of Utah; Thalia Dondero; David E. Miller, Professor of History, University of Utah; Peter Tooker; The Smithsonian Institution; William Lee Stokes, Chairman, Department of Geology, University of Utah; Tien Yang, Division of Biological Sciences, University of Arizona; U. S. Park Service.

Additional Reading

The reader may wish to refer to the following NATIONAL GEOGRAPHIC articles for additional reading and to check the *National Geographic Index* for other related material:

William Belknap, Jr., "Shooting Rapids in Reverse! Jet Boats Climb the Colorado's Torrent Through the Grand Canyon," April 1962; Walter Meayers Edwards, "Lake Powell: Waterway to Desert Wonders," July 1967; Rowe Findley, "Canyonlands, Realm of Rock and the Far Horizon," July 1971, and "Death Valley, the Land and the Legend," January 1970; Joseph Judge, "Retracing John Wesley Powell's Historic Voyage Down the Grand Canyon," May 1969; Nathaniel T. Kenney, "Big Bend, Jewel in the Texas Desert," January 1968; Robert Laxalt, "New Mexico: The Golden Land," September 1970; Jon Schneeberger, "Escalante Canyon—Wilderness at the Crossroads," August 1972.

The reader may also wish to refer to the following books:

Edward Abbey, *Desert Solitaire;* Lyman Benson, *Cacti of Arizona* and *Southwestern Desert Trees and Shrubs;* Ray Allen Billington, *The Far Western Frontier;* Ross Calvin, *Sky Determines;* J. Frank Dobie, *Coronado's Children* and *The Voice of the Coyote;* Erna Fergusson, *Our Southwest;* William H. Goetzmann, *Exploration and Empire;* James Rodney Hastings and Raymond Turner, *The Changing Mile;* W. Eugene Hollon, *The Southwest: Old and New;* Arthur Holmes, *Principles of Physical Geology;* Edmund C. Jaeger, *The California Deserts* and *The North American Deserts;* Joseph Wood Krutch, *The Desert Year, The Forgotten Peninsula,* and *The Voice of the Desert;* Peggy Larson, *Deserts of America;* Stanley Paher, *Nevada Ghost Towns and Mining Camps;* Knut Schmidt-Nielsen, *Desert Animals;* Mark Twain, *Roughing It;* T. H. Watkins, *Gold and Silver in the West.*

Composition for *Great American Deserts* by National Geographic's Phototypographic Division, Carl M. Shrader, Chief; Lawrence F. Ludwig, Assistant Chief. Printed and bound by Fawcett Printing Corp., Rockville, Md. Color separations by Beck Engraving Co., Philadelphia, Pa.; Chanticleer Company, Inc., New York; Colorgraphics, Inc., Beltsville, Md.; Graphic Color Plate, Inc., Stamford, Conn.; The Lanman Company, Alexandria, Va.; Lebanon Valley Offset Company, Inc., Annville, Pa.; Progressive Color Corp., Rockville, Md.

NATIONAL GEOGRAPHIC MAGAZINE

MELVILLE BELL GROSVENOR Editor-in-Chief and Board Chairman
MELVIN M. PAYNE President of the Society

GILBERT M. GROSVENOR Editor

FRANC SHOR, JOHN SCOFIELD Associate Editors

Senior Assistant Editors
Allan C. Fisher, Jr., Kenneth MacLeish, Robert L. Conly, W. E. Garrett

Assistant Editors: Jules B. Billard, Andrew H. Brown, James Cerruti, Edward J. Linehan, Carolyn Bennett Patterson, Howell Walker, Kenneth F. Weaver

Senior Editorial Staff: William S. Ellis, Rowe Findley, William Graves, Robert P. Jordan, Joseph Judge, Nathaniel T. Kenney, Samuel W. Matthews, Bart McDowell; Senior Scientist: Paul A. Zahl

Foreign Editorial Staff: Luis Marden (Chief); Thomas J. Abercrombie, David S. Boyer, Howard La Fay, Volkmar Wentzel, Peter T. White

Editorial Staff: Harvey Arden, Kent Britt, Thomas Y. Canby, Louis de la Haba, Mike W. Edwards, Noel Grove, Alice J. Hall, Werner Janney, Jerry Kline, John L. McIntosh, Elizabeth A. Moize, Ethel A. Starbird, Gordon Young

Editorial Layout: Howard E. Paine (Chief); Charles C. Uhl, John M. Lavery

Geographic Art: William N. Palmstrom (Chief). *Artists:* Peter V. Bianchi, Lisa Biganzoli, William H. Bond, John W. Lothers, Robert C. Magis, Robert W. Nicholson, Ned M. Seidler. *Cartographic Artists:* Victor J. Kelley, Snejinka Stefanoff. *Research:* Walter Q. Crowe (Supervisor), Virginia L. Baza, George W. Beatty, John D. Garst, Jean B. McConville, Dorothy A. Nicholson, Isaac Ortiz (Production). Marie L. Barnes (Administrative Assistant)

Editorial Research: Margaret G. Bledsoe (Chief); Ann K. Wendt (Associate Chief), Alice M. Bowsher, Jan Holderness, Levenia Loder, Frances H. Parker

Geographic Research: George Crossette (Chief); Newton V. Blakeslee (Assistant Chief), Carolyn H. Anderson, Leon J. Canova, Bette Joan Goss, Lesley B. Lane

Library: Virginia Carter Hills (Librarian); Patricia Murphy Smith (Assistant Librarian), Melba Barnes, Louise A. Robinson, Esther Ann Manion (Librarian Emeritus)

Editorial Administration: Joyce W. McKean, Assistant to the Editor; Virginia H. Finnegan, Winifred M. Myers, Shirley Neff, Inez D. Wilkinson (Editorial Assistants); Dorothy M. Corson (Indexes); Rosalie K. Millerd, Lorine Wendling (Files); Evelyn Fox, Dolores Kennedy (Transportation); Carolyn F. Clewell (Correspondence); Jeanne S. Duiker (Archives)

ILLUSTRATIONS STAFF: *Illustrations Editor:* Herbert S. Wilburn, Jr. *Associate Illustrations Editor:* Thomas R. Smith. *Art Editor:* Andrew Poggenpohl. *Assistant Illustrations Editors:* Mary Griswold Smith, O. Louis Mazzatenta, Charlene Murphy, Robert S. Patton. *Layout and Production:* H. Edward Kim (Chief). *Picture Editors:* David L. Arnold, Michael E. Long, Bruce A. McElfresh, Elie S. Rogers, W. Allan Royce, Jon Schneeberger. *Research:* Paula C. Simmons. Barbara A. Shattuck (Asst.). *Librarian:* L. Fern Dame

Engraving and Printing: Dee J. Andella (Chief); John R. Metcalfe, William W. Smith, James R. Whitney

PHOTOGRAPHIC STAFF: *Director of Photography:* Robert E. Gilka. *Assistant Directors:* Dean Conger, Joseph J. Scherschel. *Photographers:* James L. Amos, James P. Blair, Bruce Dale, Dick Durrance II, Gordon W. Gahan, Otis Imboden, Emory Kristof, Bates Littlehales, George F. Mobley, Robert S. Oakes, Winfield Parks, Robert F. Sisson (Natural Science); James L. Stanfield. Lilian Davidson (Administration). *Film Review:* Guy W. Starling (Chief). *Photographic Equipment:* John E. Fletcher (Chief), Donald McBain. *Pictorial Research:* Walter Meayers Edwards (Chief). *Photographic Laboratories and Phototypography:* Carl M. Shrader (Chief); Milton A. Ford (Associate Chief); Herbert Altemus, Jr., David H. Chisman, Lawrence F. Ludwig (Assistant Chief, Phototypography), Claude E. Petrone, J. Frank Pyles, Jr., Donald E. Stemper, George V. White

RELATED EDUCATIONAL SERVICES OF THE SOCIETY

Cartography: William T. Peele (Chief); David W. Cook (Assistant Chief). *Cartographic Staff:* Margery K. Barkdull, Charles F. Case, Ted Dachtera, Richard J. Darley, John F. Dorr, Russel G. Fritz, Richard R. Furno, Charles W. Gotthardt, Jr., Catherine M. Hart, Donald A. Jaeger, Harry D. Kauhane, James W. Killion, Manuela G. Kogutowicz, Charles L. Miller, David L. Moore, Robert W. Northrop, Richard K. Rogers, John F. Shupe, Charles L. Stern, Douglas A. Strobel, George E. Stuart (Archeology), Tibor G. Toth, Thomas A. Wall, Thomas A. Walsh

Books: Merle Severy (Chief); Seymour L. Fishbein (Assistant Chief), Thomas B. Allen, Ross Bennett, Charles O. Hyman, Anne Dirkes Kobor, John J. Putman, David F. Robinson, Wilhelm R. Saake, Verla Lee Smith

Special Publications and Educational Filmstrips: Robert L. Breeden (Chief); Donald J. Crump (Asst. Chief), Josephine B. Bolt, David R. Bridge, Linda Bridge, Margery G. Dunn, Johanna G. Farren, Ronald Fisher, Mary Ann Harrell, Bryan Hodgson, Margaret McKelway Johnson, Geraldine Linder, Robert Messer, Cynthia Ramsay, Philip B. Silcott, Joseph A. Taney

School Service: Ralph Gray (Chief and Editor of National Geographic School Bulletin); Arthur P. Miller, Jr. (Assistant Chief and Associate Editor of School Bulletin). Joseph B. Goodwin, Ellen Joan Hurst, Charles H. Sloan, Janis Knudsen Wheat

News Service: Windsor P. Booth (Chief); Paul Sampson (Assistant Chief), Donald J. Frederick, William J. O'Neill, Robert C. Radcliffe; Isabel Clarke

Television: Dennis B. Kane (Chief); David Cooper, Carl W. Harmon, Jr., Sidney Platt, Patricia F. Northrop (Administrative Assistant), Marjorie M. Moomey (Research)

Lectures: Joanne M. Hess (Chief); Robert G. Fleegal, Mary W. McKinney, Gerald L. Wiley, Carl E. Ziebe

Explorers Hall: T. Keilor Bentley (Curator-Director)

EUROPEAN OFFICES: W. Edward Roscher (Associate Secretary and Director), Jennifer Moseley (Assistant), 4 Curzon Place, Mayfair, London, W1Y 8EN, England; Jacques Ostier, 6 rue des Petits-Pères, 75-Paris 2e, France

ADVERTISING: *Director:* William A. Boeger, Jr. *National Advertising Manager:* William Turgeon, 1251 Ave. of the Americas, New York, N.Y. 10020. *Regional managers—Eastern:* George W. Kellner, New York. *Midwestern:* Robert R. Henn, Chicago. *Western:* Thomas Martz, San Francisco. *Los Angeles:* Jack Wallace. *Canada:* Robert W. Horan, New York. *Automotive:* John F. Grant, New York. *Travel:* Gerald A. Van Splinter, New York. *International Director:* James L. Till, New York. *European Director:* Richard V. Macy, 21 rue Jean-Mermoz, Paris 8e, France. *Production:* E. M. Pusey, Jr.